Maps for the local historian
A guide to the British sources
by J B Harley

Reprinted from *The Local Historian*

Published for
The Standing Conference for Local History
by the Bedford Square Press of the National
Council of Social Service 26 Bedford Square
London WC1B 3HU

© NCSS and J B Harley London 1972
reprinted 1977
ISBN 0 7199 0834 5

Printed in England by Blackfriars Press Limited, Leicester

Contents

Contents

Preface

Maps and plans are one of the most ubiquitous of all British documents in the post-medieval period. *The British Museum Catalogue of Printed Maps, Charts and Plans* (1967) runs to fifteen large volumes, but lists only a tiny fragment of the national riches of printed—leave alone manuscript—maps and plans. Few libraries are without a map collection and the cartographic content of local record offices is often as valuable as that of better-known national institutions. Maps are also one of the most varied of the major classes of historical evidence. Cartography has had an application to so many branches of human activity—both practical and intellectual—that a classification of maps is likely to have almost as many sub-divisions as a classification of books. Insofar as they vary in purpose, in date, in physical form, in detail and in accuracy, their application in the reconstruction of the past is correspondingly wide. There is an obvious need for a simple guide to assist all those who use 'old maps' in the course of their work.

The relevance of map evidence to historical studies is of course influenced as much by the specialist nature of these studies as by the availability and characteristics of the cartographic sources. Maps may range from being the one and only mode of expression of an historical fact to a situation where they merely supplement more important types of evidence. In the present *Guide*, however, such distinctions are ignored, and the basic aim is to provide a short commentary around the substantial, yet scattered, reading on the history of British maps and to single out books and articles which will assist in either the location or in the interpretation of particular groups of maps and plans. Information about published bibliographies and lists of maps and plans is concentrated at the beginning of each chapter and is followed by an account of such secondary literature as contains important background information. 'Maps', one historian has remarked, 'are a dangerous type of evidence' and, as well as being familiar with their diversity, we need to sustain a critical attitude on the question of reliability. This is likely to be determined by factors related not only to the original purpose of the map, but also to the methods by which cartographers worked. Early maps were the creation in varying degrees of tradesmen as well as craftsmen, and of artists as much as scientific surveyors. The local historian needs a working acquaintance with the detailed studies of historians of cartography—although at first sight they may seem to be forbiddingly biographical, technical, bibliographical or even antiquarian—and at the same time to adopt the ways of testing maps (as against other types of topographical evidence) developed by other scholars. This is the justification for the 'bibliographical' approach of the present publication.

This is in any case of an interim nature. The material it contains appeared as a series of articles in *The Local Historian* between 1967 and 1969 and it is reprinted from the standing type with only minor corrections. In area the treatment is confined to Great Britain, and six major categories of maps—town plans, estate plans, enclosure and tithe award plans, maps of communications, marine charts and county maps—are traced from their origins to approximately the mid-nineteenth century. The maps of the Ordnance Survey, the subject of a separate study uniform with this booklet,[1] are excluded. When the original articles were commissioned it was intended to add new sections before publication in booklet form, but, in practice, to have covered other specialist maps and plans in the same detail—such as the military plans which are mentioned *en passant*—would have greatly extended its scope. A bibliographical postscript has, however, been added to list items published since the articles were written.

J B HARLEY   Department of Geography
                                                    University of Exeter
                                                    December 1971

[1] J. B. Harley and C. W. Phillips, *The Historian's Guide to Ordnance Survey Maps* (NCSS, 1964).

1 Maps and plans of towns

Maps and plans[1] provide important evidence of the stages and processes of topographical change in towns—an environment where such changes may be both rapid and complex. But urban maps and plans, though numerous in aggregate, are uneven in local availability. The cartographic annals of one town frequently fail to match those of a neighbour—a fact influenced not only by the multiple circumstances in which maps were made, by the lottery of the survival processes, but also, in a practical sense, by the ease with which they are accessible to students. But locating a map is only the start of the historian's task. He must also assess its accuracy. Early town plans (like early maps in general) can seldom be accepted at their face value. They are of varying accuracy, according to circumstances such as the purpose of the survey, its scale, the techniques by which it was made, and, if printed, its publication history. These variables will need to be carefully considered, and the rôle of maps in contemporary history examined, if town plans are to be subjected to an adequate degree of critical scrutiny.

BIBLIOGRAPHIES AND FACSIMILES OF TOWN PLANS

In the case of town plans there is a marked disparity between our knowledge of printed and manuscript versions. Quite obviously the more widely disseminated published plan will be the better known. Moreover, the majority of published bibliographies are devoted to printed plans. Not until the nineteenth century—when lithographic processes effected a revolution in the ease and accuracy of graphical communication—do more town maps come within the scope of existing bibliography. Bearing this in mind, the best starting point in seeking the maps and plans of any British town is usually in its Public Library or Archives. Not surprisingly, local municipal libraries have

[1] By Ordnance Survey definition a 'plan' is at a sufficiently large scale for all topographical features to be shown to true scale. Quite obviously many early town 'plans' fail to meet this requirement so that here the word is used loosely to denote a large-scale, detailed map.

had especial opportunities (and a vested interest) in the collection of local maps. Some have acquired important privately-owned collections relating to the town and its environs—such as the Thomas Binns' collection in the City of Liverpool Record Office or the outstandingly valuable Fairbank collection in Sheffield City Library—and many have large holdings of urban maps and plans—both printed and manuscript. The researcher who can visit a local library will be well served (in the main) by either lists or card-index catalogues, some of which may be arranged by publisher, surveyor, engraver and subject.

On the other hand, the *published* finding-aids may be less than adequate. There is no general account of the development of British town plans although Angela Fordham's *Town Plans of the British Isles* (Map Collectors' Series No. 22) reproduces a selection of forty of the more decorative varieties. In the field of printed bibliography the photo-lithographic edition of *The British Museum Catalogue of Printed Maps, Charts and Plans* (15 Vols., 1967) contains, for numerous towns, the most useful general list of the range of available plans, and of printed topographical views and prospects (although many manuscript plans occur in the catalogues of the Department of Manuscripts). Otherwise, we have to turn to the rather meagre crop of publications about the early maps of particular towns. These are of two main types. First, there are descriptive bibliographies of historical maps (of varying detail and usually listing general printed maps rather than specialised plans); and, second, there are facsimile editions of town plans.

Only a handful of British towns are well served in both respects, which would suggest, that until recently, maps have been a cinderella amongst urban records. London is one of the exceptions. The local historian can refer not only to the authoritative *Printed Maps of London circa 1553-1850* (1964), a bibliography by Ida Darlington and James Howgego, but also consult facsimiles of many important plans—notably those issued by the London Topographical Society. The early plans of Bristol have been discussed by John E. Pritchard, especially in his 'Old Plans and Views of Bristol', *Trans. Bristol and Glos. Arch. Soc.* Vol. XLVIII (1928); and facsimiles have been issued in the same Society's A *Gloucestershire and Bristol Atlas* (1961); and by the Bristol City Museum. Manchester Public Libraries also publish facsimiles of several town plans, which are described in J. Lee's *Maps and Plans of Manchester and Salford, 1650-1843* (1957). But as a publication deliberately designed to help the local historian *Southampton Maps from Elizabethan Times* (Southampton Corporation, 1964), twenty-four facsimiles introduced by Edwin Welch, could be a model to other towns; and, of the few bibliographies embracing both general and specialised town plans, the *Printed Maps and Plans of Leeds, 1711-1900* (Thoresby Society, 1960) by Kenneth J. Bonser and Harold Nichols is of more than local interest: it is a conspectus of the range of cartographic evidence available for the larger English town.

Scotland is better equipped than England in terms of published bibliography. In *The Early Maps of Scotland* (R.S.G.S., 1936) the section on 'The Town Plans of Scotland' listed the materials known to the compilers (a revised edition is in preparation). The maps of Edinburgh are treated in *The Early Views and Maps of Edinburgh, 1544-1852* (R.S.G.S., 1919) and in William Cowan's *The Maps of Edinburgh, 1544-1929* (Edinburgh Public Libraries, 1932).

Finally, the researcher may have to cast his net much more widely for a particular town plan. Rare copies may be scattered in any of the record repositories in which maps are found; and, sometimes, they can be traced through the circulated lists of the National Register of Archives. Naturally, the larger national map collections, including those of the British Museum, the Public Record Office—whose plans are now listed in *Maps and Plans in the Public Record Office, I. British Isles, c. 1410-1860* (1967)—the Bodleian and Cambridge University Libraries, the National Libraries of Wales and Scotland, and the Royal Geographical Society, have substantial collections which should be checked as a first step. But less widely-known institutions may contain a crucial map. Just as there is no end to the making of maps, so, too, for the local historian there may be no easy end to the systematic search for these valuable documents.

GENERAL TOWN PLANS

A major group of town plans share the common attribute that they depict the whole area of the town for a particular date. Not only do they give a period picture of the face of a town; but, where a sequence of these maps exists, they record the stages of town growth. They may be conveniently classified within major time periods.

Tudor bird's-eye view plans

The art of depicting towns accurately in plan, if known to the Romans, was lost to the Middle Ages. In medieval manuscripts, the artist often portrayed stylised drawings of cities, such as those in the early maps of the British Isles prepared by Mathew Paris (c. A.D. 1250), or in the Gough Map (of c. A.D. 1360). They were merely pictorial drawings, emphasising a few buildings, but taking no account of true ground plan. The bird's eye view—the earliest stage in the evolution of the town plan proper—did not develop until Tudor times. Even then, the horizontal scale of these plans varied in accuracy, although they do show the main buildings, bridges, trees, hedges and hills in elevation, and figures—illustrating the day-to-day life of the urban community—populate the landscape as in a painting.

Relatively few of these plans were engraved. As we might expect, London was the object of more frequent mapping and its Elizabethan cartography is

FIGURE 1. The town plans in John Speed's *The Theatre of the Empire of Great Britaine* (1612). Plans of the towns indicated in capital letters had already been published in the *Civitates Orbis Terrarum* by Braun and Hogenberg.

illustrated in Stephen Powys Marks, *The Map of Mid-Sixteenth Century London* (L.T.S., 1964). Plans were also engraved of the more important provincial towns—such as York, Bristol and Norwich—but the greater number remained in manuscript. The plan of Chelmsford (1591)—reproduced in F. G. Emmison's *Catalogue of Maps in the Essex Record Office* . . . (1947)—or the plan of Sherborne (Dorset)—described by P. D. A. Harvey in 'An Elizabethan Map of Manors in North Dorset', *The British Museum Quarterly* Vol. XXIX (1965)—were both of small country towns delineated in the course of a rural estate survey, and such plans are to be located in estate-paper collections. A further source of early bird's-eye view plans is in the marine charts of the period. Examples are reproduced in A. H. W. Robinson's *Marine Cartography in Britain* (1962), and others exist, notably in the hydrographic collections of the British Museum and in the National Maritime Museum at Greenwich. They may be distorted, however, to bring into prominence features easily recognisable at sea; and emphasis is often on harbours and adjacent fortifications rather than on the town as a whole. The same may be true of sketch plans of towns designed for military purposes, as the earliest perspective plan of Edinburgh, made for the army of the Earl of Hertford in 1544.

Thus, in one way or another, many British towns had been mapped by 1600, but the initiative in collecting and publishing an urban atlas came from Europe. The 1550 edition of Sebastian Munster's *Cosmographia* contained woodcut views of Edinburgh and London; it was modest in conception by the side of Braun and Hogenberg's *Civitates Orbis Terrarum* (now—1966—reproduced in facsimile with an introduction by R. A. Skelton), the first five volumes of which (1572-1598) included a selection of oblique and bird's-eye views of British towns supplied by English plan makers such as William Smith (see Figure 1). The attempt to publish a similar collection of the plans of English towns to accompany Holinshed's *Chronicles* (1577) did not materialise.

In this period (and subsequently) the panoramic view was closely allied to the town plan. Indeed, in the sixteenth and seventeenth centuries, it is sometimes difficult to distinguish between the two formats, which give inter-related evidence about the extent of the town; and, on detailed 'prospects', the architecture of individual buildings; Shakespearean scholars have used Cornelius Visscher's engraved Long View of London (1616) to reconstruct the plan of the Globe Theatre. There is an account of 'Pre-fire Panoramas' in the *Printed Maps of London circa 1553-1850*, and, if the corresponding record of provincial towns is less rich, it is seldom lacking, and can throw definite light on the contemporary face of many towns.

The town plans of John Speed

A major landmark in cartography was the inclusion by John Speed of town plans and views as insets to the county maps in *The Theatre of the*

Empire of Great Britaine . . . (1612). No less than seventy-three places were portrayed. Although John Norden had already introduced the inset town plan to the county map, Speed's was the first systematic collection of British town plans, and, moreover, contains the earliest printed plans of many towns (see Figure 1). In terms of cartographical technique they embody the transition from the older bird's-eye view to the modern two-dimensional plan—for Speed improved on the work of his predecessors. An essential aid to their interpretation is R. A. Skelton's 'Tudor Town Plans in John Speed's *Theatre*', *The Archaeological Journal* Vol. CVIII (1952): here the local historian is given an object lesson in the critical examination of maps. Only about a quarter of Speed's plans were derived from earlier sources; the remainder originated (as he tells us) during his 'owne travels' and these were distinguished by 'The Scale of Pases' inserted in forty-five cases. Even so, all need to be interpreted cautiously. The topography should be collated with accurate modern plans, and the limitations of scale (necessitating the omission of detail) and of technique be recognised.

Speed's plans create additional pitfalls for the unwary insofar as they were frequently republished, without modification, for the next century and a half. They persist not only in later editions of the *Theatre* (up to 1770); but, after c. 1690, they appear as insets in Philip Lea's edition of Saxton's *The Shires of England and Wales* (which was also reprinted up to c. 1770). Furthermore, just as the British town plans in Braun and Hogenberg were reproduced as sketch miniatures in Francesco Valeso's *Raccolta di le piu illustri et famose citta di tutto il mondo* (Venice, 1595) so, too (to cite but one example), the town plans in the *Britannia Magna* (1661) by Rutger Hermannides were based almost entirely on Speed. We must be on our guard against the anachronism of these versions.

The late seventeenth and the eighteenth century

After Speed's *Theatre* there tends to be a gap in the cartographic documentation of many towns. We can, however, see the seeds of improvement sprouting in the work of John Ogilby (died 1676). His famous map of London was published posthumously by William Morgan, and, in the road book *Britannia* (1675), he made the attempt to show 'Capital Towns . . . Ichnographically*, according to their Form and Extent'—that is, in two dimensions. Its intended complement, a 'Description of the 25 Cities with Peculiar Charts to each of them', never materialised, and substantial progress in the mapping of towns awaited the eighteenth century. Thereafter the two-dimensional plan became ubiquitous as the Georgian spate of urban building was matched by a flood of new maps. Most existing towns were re-surveyed once (and often more) in this century. In many cases the plans were at unprecedented scales (sometimes sufficiently detailed to show the subdivision of the town into

12

burgage plots), and are a vital link in reconstructing medieval topography. The cartographers were often local land surveyors, such as William Fairbank who mapped Sheffield (1771), or William Green, whose plan of Manchester and Salford (1794) has also become a standard topographical document. But others were London map-makers with a national reputation. John Rocque, for instance, was active in mapping towns (as well as estates and counties) and published plans of Bristol (1742), Exeter (1744), Shrewsbury (1746) and London (1746), as well as A Collection of Plans of the Principal Cities of Great Britain and Ireland . . . (1764) issued in partnership with Andrew Dury.

Many eighteenth-century town plans were insets in the new county maps of the period 1750-1800. Benjamin Donn's map of Devon (1765) included plans of Exeter and Plymouth, while Thomas Jefferys, Geographer to the King, had town surveys made for his series of county maps: Yorkshire (1771-72) had larger-scale inset plans of Ripon, Kingston upon Hull, Sheffield, Leeds, York and Scarborough. However, these plans are sometimes out-of-date compared with the main map. A contemporary noted that the plan of Wells in John Strachey's map of Somerset (1736) was undertaken by a surveyor 'when a schoolboy by Inspection without measure or Instrumt'; and the plan of Leicester, in the otherwise excellent map of Leicestershire by John Prior (1779), was an inferior and unrevised adaptation of Samuel Carte's map of 1722.

We should also remember that a large number of town plans were not published in independent sheet form but were illustrations in books. One of the best plans of Georgian Liverpool—the 'Plan of the Town and Port of Liverpool' (1769) by George Perry — was associated with his History of Leverpool published by William Enfield (1769). Indeed, many urban historians, in company with the compilers of guide books and directories, adhered to the practice of including town plans (sometimes especially surveyed) in their works. Nor did the vogue for publishing 'prospects' of towns—often from several viewpoints—decline. In the seventeenth century the town plans of Wenceslaus Hollar were accompanied by views taken from a low elevation; and, in the following century, the prospects of towns by Samuel Buck—he engraved eighty-three views of the main cities and towns in England and Wales—characterise a common form of topographical evidence, which can add considerably to our knowledge of urban geography. All in all, the cartographic evidence for British towns circa 1800 was much more abundant than a century earlier.

The nineteenth century

Rapid town growth—especially in the railway age—made even greater demands on cartographers. Up to c. 1840, town plans continued in their traditional formats. Original sheet maps continued to be made by private

13

enterprise; such was William Shakeshaft's plan of Preston (1809), at a scale of c. 20 inches to one mile, described in the *Lancashire Record Office Report for 1964*. These maps often show proposed as well as existing town development. In the case of Jonathan Bennison's Map of Liverpool (1835) proposed streets are aligned along the enclosed strips of the town fields (Plate 1); here, as in many towns, these plans spell out the piecemeal sale of pre-existing plots which influenced the pattern of the developing urban landscape.

As earlier, several collections of town plans were published. *The British Atlas* . . . (1810) by J. Cole and J. Roper contained twenty-one plans, but some, at least, were obsolete having originally been engraved to accompany *The Beauties of England and Wales* by E. W. Brayley and J. Britton, which began publication in 1801, and was itself a secondary compilation. Two collections of town plans, derived from the Ordnance Survey by R. K. Dawson, accompanied the enquiries into municipal government in the 1830s. The first, *Plans of the Cities and Boroughs of England and Wales* (1832), was only at a scale of 1" or 2" to one mile (in the comparable volume for Scotland the seventy-two plans were on a scale of 6" to one mile). But a later series of nearly 180 plans, showing ward boundaries, were enlarged to a scale of 4" to one mile in the *Report of the Municipal Corporation Boundaries Commission* . . . (1837). In this period, Scotland is also particularly well served by Wood's Town Atlas—an extensive collection of town plans by John Wood, surveyed between 1818 and 1826.

The nineteenth century also saw an increasing crop of maps and plans in gazetteers, street directories and travellers' (including railway) guide books. Town plans became more frequent in works of general reference as well as in orthodox geographical texts. In 1833 the S.D.U.K. published a two-volume atlas called *Maps of the Society for the Diffusion of Useful Knowledge*, which contained town plans of Edinburgh, Birmingham, Liverpool and London. These, and the town plans published by John Tallis and Co. Ltd. in the 1850s, are examples of a group of early Victorian plans the margins of which are distinguished by attractive views of the principal buildings.

Directory maps become particularly numerous. They accompanied some of the publications listed by Jane E. Norton in a *Guide to the National and Provincial Directories of England and Wales, excluding London, published before 1856* (1950). J. A. Pigot's Manchester directory of 1804, Edward Baines's *History, Directory & Gazetteer of the County of York* (1822-1823), and its companion volume *History, Directory & Gazetteer of the County of . . . . Lancaster* (1824-1825), were amongst the most reliable of this genre—incorporating a number of especially surveyed plans. Such high standards however were far from universal: directory compilers often inserted some (unacknowledged) earlier map; and then, subsequently, failed to revise it in phase with fresh editions of the text—despite claims for new and accurate surveys. The same dangers are endemic to the plans in guide books and similar publications;

14

but, again, there may be no alternative for their evidence. The nineteenth-century expansion of Cheltenham, for instance, is most graphically expressed in the plans in two quite unrelated books: Thomas Jameson's *A Treatise on Cheltenham Waters and Bilious Diseases* (1809) and Henry Davies' *A View of Cheltenham in its Past and Present State* (1843).

Towards mid-century large-scale accurate plans became more widely available. Two of their standard sources may be noted. First, there were town plans amongst the tithe surveys of the mid-nineteenth century. Tithe maps have probably been more widely used in studies of rural areas (see pp. 35-6), but their large scale (from 13" to 26" to one mile) provides valuable detail of built-up areas at a time of rapid change. On some tithe maps, however, urban areas were left blank. Second, from the 1840s onwards, the Ordnance Survey began publication of its series of town plans at the scales of 1/1056, 1/528 and 1/500, as well as the continuing editions of the 25" and (later) 50" maps of urban areas. The dates, revisions and availability of these plans have been described in *The Historian's Guide to Ordnance Survey Maps* (NCSS, 1964). That they are a watershed in the history of urban cartography cannot be over-stressed. Henceforth such official maps largely supplant surveys by private cartographers—although derived town plans, and interim revisions of the official editions, continued to be produced in great numbers by the commercial map publishers. Many town councils have also maintained up-to-date versions of Ordnance Survey plans which persist up to the present day; and, in many other cases they became the appropriate base on which specialised detail could be added.

SPECIALISED TOWN PLANS

A second major group of town plans often covered only part of a town. They are numerous but specialised and record aspects of urban history such as the sale of property, development schemes, new transport undertakings, and a variety of projects for public utilities: all are of potential interest. Their especial value to the local historian is in lending precise topographical definition to small areas and special features within the town. Although any classification involves a degree of overlap, these plans are perhaps most readily understood in terms of their provenance.

Plans of urban landowners

Property plans have survived from the sixteenth century onwards. A map of St. Paul's parish, Canterbury, c. 1550, owned by the Church of England, is now in the City of Canterbury Archives; and urban glebe lands were sometimes mapped as those belonging to the parsonage of Shalford (Surrey) which included a plan of Guildford (1617). Landowners' plans become common after 1700, and are a really prolific source of evidence after 1800. Some cities, such as London, Newcastle-upon-Tyne or Liverpool, where the estates of the

Municipal Corporation are extensive, have considerable numbers of property plans. The official records of the Corporation of London at Guildhall (the categories of plan are mirrored elsewhere) include plans of schools, hospitals, courts, markets, prisons, bridges, parks and other properties, and of improvement schemes of various kinds. We can glimpse their variety in Philip E. Jones and Raymond Smith, A Guide to the Records in the Corporation of London Records Office and the Guildhall Library Muniment Room (1951). In general the more ancient a city the more complex its cartographic archives may be. We must search not only for cadastral plans of Corporation properties, of lands belonging to the church, but of other ancient institutions such as the City Guilds and Livery Companies, to say nothing of the plans of properties of private individuals. By way of contrast, the basic map records (in terms of maps of ownership) of towns created in the eighteenth and nineteenth centuries may be far simpler. In the case of Huddersfield the land was owned by one family and sold to the Corporation as one unit, and, as a result, more comprehensive plans (in some cases listing tenants in an accompanying book of reference) are available for 1716, 1780 and 1825.

The plans which accompany leases and conveyances, and the numerous plans associated with sale catalogues, may also be of historical use, and for the additional written particulars they contain. Or we may have to turn to the new landowners of the nineteenth century for plan material. The railway companies, for example, built up large estates in many towns, and recorded it on special plans. The Great Western policy in urban areas was to maintain large-scale plans at forty feet to an inch depicting stations, goods yards and other railway-owned installations, and, incidentally, parts of the area in which they were located.

Housing development schemes

During the eighteenth and nineteenth centuries detailed plans for new housing were prepared by the promoters. The 'Sketch[es] of Sundry Lots of Land in Toxteth Park [Liverpool] for Sale' (c. 1798) illustrates such a speculation in real estate. The record may be detailed enough to trace the growth of suburbia estate by estate, street by street, while some plans were large enough in scale—as those of Sheffield in the Fairbank Collection (see Plate 2)—to show individual house plots set out for development: a few already built upon; others with the names of their first purchasers; and the remainder blank. An added interest to the plans of property developers—later including those of Local Councils ranging from pioneer attempts to provide artisans' dwellings to more modern layouts for garden suburbs—is that they may depict schemes which never got past the drawing board. Such were the late-eighteenth century proposals, only partly executed, to create exclusive residential estates at the Crescent in Birmingham, or the Polygon area in Southampton, to which contemporary plans provide eloquent testimony.

Some surveyors, such as Thomas Hornor—describing himself upon a plan of Kingston-upon-Thames (1813) as a 'pictural and descriptive planner of estates' —made a speciality of this work. However, such maps should also be treated cautiously as evidence of *actual* change; an over-enthusiasm to keep up-to-date tempted cartographers to anticipate housing developments, which may, in the end, have turned out differently.

Plans of public undertakings

From the late eighteenth century onwards numerous plans of public utility schemes are available, including municipal plans for gasworks, sewerage, drainage, water supply and lighting. We should not underestimate the historical interest of the plans accompanying these soundingly prosaic events in the life of a town. A private Act of Parliament was usually required for their execution; and after 1794, plans accompanying the proceedings were statutorily deposited locally and in the House of Lords Record Office (the House of Commons series begin in 1818). The categories and finding-aids for these latter plans are described by Maurice Bond in *The Records of Parliament. A Guide for Genealogists and Local Historians* (1964); and the local copies may have been deposited in the County Record Office. Detail varied, but some, such as a plan of Rochdale indicating the proposed waterworks (1809), on a scale of 24″ to a mile, may be unequalled in their period. Many were specialised in function, and thus the cartographic record of certain towns is particularly rich. The archives of ports, for example, include detailed plans of improvements to harbours, docks, ports, piers and quays. The study by Alan F. Williams of 'Bristol Port Plans and Improvement Schemes of the 18th Century', *Trans. Bristol and Glos. Arch. Soc.* Vol. 81 (1962), illuminates the richness and diversity of this type of source material, which is matched in seaside resorts by the specialised plans of pier, marine promenade and other seafront installations. There are few aspects of urban improvement in the last two centuries—the evolution of the open spaces embedded in the town (common lands, parks, gardens, golf courses and allotments); the extension of borough and ward boundaries; even the making of small-scale slum clearances or the building of factories—the history of which has not been captured in contemporary maps.

Urban transport schemes

Transport maps are dealt with in a special section of the *Guide*. We may note in the present context, however, that whenever a line of transport cut into an existing built-up area, a cartographic record of the incision may be available. Insofar as Acts of Parliament were required for major transport undertakings three copies of the plans may be available : in the local record repository; in the archives of the British Transport Commission; and in the House of Lords' Record Office. Plans illustrating street diversions and improvements are especially numerous and date from the early turnpike era down to the time of the latest urban motorways. Even where an early road (or canal) map dealt primarily with large distances on a small scale, they often include a larger-scale treatment of urban sections of the scheme. Amongst these changes (both proposed and completed) railway plans have left unusually detailed records of the nineteenth-century town. Some of those available for Leeds are enumerated in the *Printed Maps and Plans of Leeds, 1711-1900,* and indicate the possibilities for other towns. After 1853, a special type of railway plan arose out of the Railway Company's obligation to obtain Parliamentary sanction where it intended to demolish thirty or more houses in the same parish: a plan accompanying these 'Demolition Statements' is reproduced in 'Some Social Costs of Railway Building in London', by H. J. Dyos, *The Journal of Transport History,* Vol. III (1957-1958). Finally, the student of local history may find the detailed plans, sections, and books of reference which accompanied the building of tramway, omnibus, and trolley bus systems; as well as the plans of town bridges, subways and tunnels, of value in reconstructing former landscape features.

Miscellaneous maps and plans

Undoubtedly, local researchers will encounter types of town plan not mentioned above. They may be unusual because they illustrate a unique or ephemeral phase of the town's history. A special map of Preston (1715) was made to indicate the military positions at the Battle of Preston during the Jacobite Rebellion; and similar maps illustrated the defences of Carlisle and Chester at the time of the 1745 rising. Such maps of defensive installations in ports or garrison towns were the work of the military engineers of the seventeenth, eighteenth and nineteenth centuries and will be found, *inter alia,* in the map collections of the British Museum and the Public Record Office. In the mid-nineteenth century cholera epidemics prompted an unusual kind of themeatic map locating the outbreaks of disease within particular towns; they are described by E. W. Gilbert in 'Pioneer Maps of Health and Disease in England', *The Geographical Journal* Vol. CXXIV (1958). Town plans were acquiring new uses as scientific and sociological tools: on the map of 'Liverpool Ecclesiastical and Social' (1858) the Reverend A. Hume depicted 'Pauper Streets, Semi Pauper Streets, Streets of Crime & Immorality'. Likewise, an important group of urban plans were the by-product of the mid-Victorian Public Health movement; some were separate large-scale plans prepared by officers of the Royal Engineers; others depict fragments of towns and are liberally scattered in the Parliamentary Blue Books which reported on urban conditions. Hand in hand with these enquiries a whole series of changes in Local Government after 1832 (for a summary see V. D. Lipman, *Local Government Areas 1834-1945* (1949)) called for the making of accurate and detailed plans as a part of day-to-day administration. Many of these plans, once the property of Borough Engineers' Departments, or of the Town Clerk's Office, are now passing into local record offices. And, today, town planning offices are creating a whole range of new maps for historical posterity.

2 Estate maps

Estate maps are nearly always large-scale, usually manuscript up to the Ordnance Survey period, and delineate the property of one landowner. In date the main body ranges from Elizabethan to mid-Victorian times; in scope from the single map of a farm to a series depicting the lands of a large estate. Notwithstanding their uneven distribution in time and space, they form in aggregate a large and distinctive body of topographical evidence. F. G. Emmison, in *Archives and Local History* (1966), estimated there to be over 20,000 pre-1850 private estate maps in record repositories, but as new deposits are made, the total will need revision. Moreover, in any British calculation the substantial body of Scottish estate maps must be reckoned.

This is not to imply that every local historian can hope to find a detailed estate map for his area. In England, although a complete blank will seldom be drawn, roughly only one in ten estate maps covers the *whole* parish; and while many straddle lands in several parishes, they may depict only fragments of the area. In Scotland the coverage for some counties may be fuller than further south—but only for the period after 1750. At a regional level, the sample may be an adequate basis for generalisation about the unmapped residue. Yet not all counties will be as well-endowed as Kent, where A. R. H. Baker was able to locate 187 estate maps before 1700 portraying landholdings in 117 of the 400 or so parishes of the county ('Field Patterns in Seventeenth-Century Kent', *Geography* Vol. L (1965)); however, as M. W. Beresford reminds us in *History on the Ground* (1957), even a few surviving plans will 'equip the reader for other journeys into villages and fields where no early open-field map was made or where none has survived'.

BIBLIOGRAPHIES OF ESTATE MAPS

General descriptions of estate maps will be found in John West's *Village Records* (1962), F. G. Emmison's *Archives and Local History* (1966), and in two articles, 'Local History in Early Estate Maps', *Amateur Historian* Vol. 5

(1962) by A. R. H. Baker and 'Estate Maps and Surveys', *History* Vol. XLVIII (1963) by F. G. Emmison. They have been harnessed in numerous studies in the field of historical geography, but the essays in Maurice Beresford's *History on the Ground*, and in *Medieval England an Aerial Survey* (1958), by the same author and J. K. S. St Joseph, provide particularly stimulating illustrations of their potential in local studies.

The historian's proven appetite for estate maps is not sufficiently nourished by scholarly bibliography. It is a field in which Scotland has set a noteworthy precedent in the recently established *Union Catalogue of Large Scale MS. Maps of Scotland* (a short note appears in *The Cartographical Journal* Vol. 3 (1966)). The master catalogue, in the National Library of Scotland, already contains some 2,500 main entries. There is no counterpart for either England or Wales (could a plea be entered?) although the *Dictionary of Surveyors*, launched by F. W. Steer, County Archivist of West Sussex, must be noted (see 'The proposed dictionary of surveyors' *Journal of the Society of Archivists* Vol. 1 (1959)). This work is now transferred to the editorship of Mr. Peter Eden in the Department of Local History at Leicester University: its several thousand entries promise to tell us a great deal about that neglected figure in English local history—the land surveyor.

In England and Wales the County Record Offices are the principal repositories of estate maps. They often maintain detailed on-the-spot indexes: yet, although F. G. Emmison and G. H. Fowler edited a *Catalogue of Maps in the Bedfordshire County Muniments* in 1930, few counties have followed suit. Of post-war bibliographies the *Catalogue of Maps in the Essex Record Office 1566-1855* (1947—and Supplements 1952, 1964 and 1968), containing a valuable introductory essay by F. G. Emmison, remains as a model meeting the needs of the most exacting student. More recently, *A Catalogue of Sussex Estate Maps and Tithe Award Maps* by F. W. Steer (Sussex Record Society, Vol. LXI, 1962) provides exemplary coverage for the two Sussex Record Offices and the Sussex Archaeological Society (a supplementary volume including further estate maps was published in 1968). Buckinghamshire Record Society issued a *Handlist of Buckinghamshire Estate Maps* (1963), followed by *Buckinghamshire Estate Maps* (1964): the latter comprised seventeen facsimiles (the originals dating from 1444 to 1781) which are particularly welcome in view of the scarcity of such reproductions.

We should not overlook less detailed finding-aids. The general *Guides* to County Record Offices, such as those published for Bedfordshire (1957)—where the information on maps is conveniently concentrated—for Kent (1958), Nottinghamshire (1960), and Lancashire (1962), refer briefly to estate plans, as do published catalogues of individual manuscript collections: *The Guide to the Russell Estate Collections for Bedfordshire and Devon to 1910* (Bedfordshire Record Office, 1966), for example, mentions over a hundred estate maps. Of particular utility are the Reports of the National Register of

21

Archives,[1] now describing several thousand deposited manuscript collections, though not of course all containing maps or all located in County Record Offices. Indeed, these lists underline the wide dispersion of estate maps: in the archives of cities which possessed rural estates; in the muniment rooms of Oxford and Cambridge Colleges; in other ancient institutions such as St. Bartholomew's Hospital, whose large collection includes plans by the Elizabethan surveyor Ralph Treswell; in solicitors' offices; and in private collections —especially in Scotland.

The estate maps in the national repositories can be more easily traced. Manuscript maps occur in several collections of the British Museum; and as well as various indexes in the Map Room and an index of maps and surveys in the Manuscripts Room, we may consult the *Catalogue of the Manuscript Maps, Charts and Plans . . . in the British Museum* (3 Vols. 1844-61; reprinted 1962) and the various *Catalogues of Additions to Manuscripts*. For the Public Record Office we may turn to *Maps and Plans in the Public Record Office I. British Isles c. 1410-1860* (1967); and, for a first instalment of its extensive cartographic riches, to the *Descriptive List of Plans in the Scottish Record Office* Vol. 1 (1966). There are, however, no printed catalogues of the maps in the National Library of Wales, in the Bodleian or in Cambridge University Libraries, although guidance as to the manuscript maps of the last two will be found in their respective *Summary Catalogues of Western MSS.*

THE DEVELOPMENT OF ESTATE MAPS

Apart from general texts on the history of cartography[2] the catalogues of the periodic exhibitions under the auspices of the Royal Institution of Chartered Surveyors provide particularly useful background material on the history of local map-making. They include *Seven Centuries of Surveying in Suffolk* (1954), *Surveyors and Map-Makers* (1955) about Yorkshire, and *The Story of Surrey in Maps* (1956). The historian may expect to find many parallels between the changes epitomised in these pamphlets and his own area, which are necessary to evaluate his local cartography with critical insight.

Medieval Estate Maps

Medieval land surveying was concerned primarily with written rather than graphic description, and with valuation rather than exact measurement, which indeed, in the modern sense, was beyond the skill of the medieval surveyor (see E. G. R. Taylor, 'The Surveyor' *Economic History Review* Vol. XVII (1947)). Rentals, extents, terriers and charters—the documentary fruits of medieval surveying—were sometimes so detailed as to recite each holding in the village fields, but were not usually accompanied by maps. Yet

[1] Unfortunately the circulation of *complete* sets of these lists is confined to the five copyright libraries in England, Wales and Scotland, to the Public Record Office of Northern Ireland, Belfast, the Scottish Record Office, Edinburgh, the Institute of Historical Research in the University of London, and the John Rylands Library, Manchester.

[2] See pp. 77-8.

we must make a modest claim for the medieval map maker. Primitive plans were occasionally made and are discussed by Derek J. Price in 'Medieval Land Surveying and Topographical Maps', *Geographical Journal* Vol. CXXXI (1955). As later, they sometimes illustrated land disputes, such as the Kirkstead Psalter plan, drawn c.1300, relating to a twelfth-century dispute over the common cow-pastures of Kirkstead and Revesby. After 1400 an increasing knowledge of map drawing is discernible. However, as the plan of the demesne of Chertsey Abbey (1432)—reproduced by R. A. Skelton in 'Colour in Mapmaking', *The Geographical Magazine* Vol. XXXII (1960)—or of Boarstall (1444)— reproduced by Buckinghamshire Record Society — illustrate, these plans were not yet based on mathematical survey. Scale could vary on one map, and the emphasis on exaggerated perspective drawings—at Chertsey of the Abbey church, its barn and watermills—added to the general distortion.

Such maps are rare, perhaps a score have survived, but the high mortality of documents urges us not to be dogmatic about the numbers which were originally made. Subsequent improvements in early-sixteenth century plans, such as those of the Duchy of Lancaster described by E. M. Yates in *The Geographical Journal* Vol. 127 (1961) and *The Agricultural History Review* Vol. XII (1964), also hint at evolution rather than the sudden importation of a new cartographic tradition; indeed, the administrators of this estate may have gradually pioneered the use of local maps in legal disputes.

Estate maps of the sixteenth and seventeenth centuries

After 1550 there was a revolution in local cartography. 'Within ten years of Elizabeth's accession', E. G. R. Taylor writes in *The Mathematical Practitioners of Tudor and Stuart England* (1954), 'geometrical methods of estate survey . . . had become well established, and the simple "land meater" carrying a perch rod or a knotted cord . . . was replaced by the professional surveyor able to prepare a well executed and ornamented estate plan'. Precise and detailed estate maps *rose to supplement* but *not to supersede* the traditional written surveys. It is probable, as Eric Kerridge emphasises in 'The Manorial Survey as an Historical Source', *The Amateur Historian* Vol. 7 (1966), that maps were first made only when an exceptionally clear definition of land was required—as with enclosures or legal disputes—where a plan would help the litigants to unravel the complexities of local geography. But these cases were sufficiently numerous to obtain recognition for the new cartography. Land surveyors were increasingly employed by landowners from the Crown downwards. The re-distribution of church lands in the sixteenth century, the consolidation and exchange of openfield strips, the improvement of estates, and the changing ownership of land during the Commonwealth and at the Restoration, are all reflected in the output of estate maps. Nor should we forget, as H. C. Darby has pointed out in 'The Agrarian Contribution to Surveying in England', *Geographical Journal* Vol. LXXXII (1933), that the land surveyor was often a positive propagandist of rural improvement, not

23

merely a passive technician: the historian must consider him as a factor in change, as well as seeking his evidence.

Estate maps began to develop a uniformity of design transcending differences in date and place, but not always obscuring the idiosyncracies of individual presentation. The early textbooks on surveying by men such as Ralph Agas, John Norden and Aaron Rathborne helped to standardise field-survey techniques. The imitation of engraved county maps by some of the highly qualified estate surveyors went some way to ironing out parochial differences in style. Of especial importance, the land surveyor was a peripatetic craftsman in the service of the great landowner: the distances he travelled and the speed at which he worked was remarkable. This disseminated new ideas about estate mapping: it also produced some of our finest carto-graphic records. The Sussex maps accompanying the *Buckhurst Terrier* 1597-1598 (Sussex Record Society, Vol. XXXIX, 1933); the maps of the properties of All Souls College made in the 1580s (see Maurice Beresford, *op. cit.*, 1957); and the early-seventeenth century maps of the demesnes of Henry Percy, Earl of Northumberland, surveyed by Robert Norton (see the village maps derived from these by R. A. Butlin in 'Northumberland Field Systems', *The Agricultural History Review*, Vol. XII, 1964) all illustrate the importance of patronage in the development of estate mapping. Not sur-prisingly, the men who undertook these surveys crop up elsewhere in the history of cartography: John Norden, Philip Symonson and Christopher Saxton turned easily from the mapping of a county or town, to that of an estate. Estate maps by Saxton are discussed by G. R. Batho and W. R. Serjeant in the *Geographical Journal* (Vol. 125, 1959 and 132, 1966, respectively); and a group of Norden's manuscript surveys are reproduced in *Orford Ness, a Selection of Maps mainly by John Norden* (1966).

The Hanoverian period

1700 to 1850 was the golden age of the local land surveyor. Changes in country and town required maps in unprecedented number and variety. The surveyor branched out into new enterprises, as well as remaining a key figure in rural estate management. The Ordnance Survey offered little competition until after 1850, and this was a profitable era for the professional surveyor. A spate of new surveying textbooks often went into several editions—such as John Love's *Geodaesia* (1st Ed. 1688; 13th ed., 1796). The London craftsmen—who by 1800 enjoyed European pre-eminence—were manufacturing more precise surveying instruments. Methods of presentation were improved. Pre-1700 estate maps were sometimes crude in execution and exaggerated perspec-tive drawings were still fairly common: thereafter, more sophisticated draughtsmanship and decoration became normal. Contemplating such maps we sense the surveyor's pride in his craft. The standards which were reached are nowhere better demonstrated than in the ambitious manuscript and engraved surveys of the Goodwood estates, undertaken by Yeakell and

Gardner in the late-eighteenth century for the Duke of Richmond. They are preserved in fourteen splendid volumes in the Sussex Record Office (see F. W. Steer, *op. cit.* and R. A. Skelton, 'The Origins of the Ordnance Survey of Great Britain', *Geographical Journal* Vol. CXXVIII, 1962). In the early nineteenth century the invention of lithography presented another opportunity: instead of the slow labour of hand copying—often the task of an apprentice surveyor—cheap and accurate multiple copies could be made. Lithographed estate plans became common during the nineteenth century.

The output of Hanoverian estate maps was therefore large, not only in lowland England, but also in hitherto poorly surveyed regions. Scotland became the scene of much detailed mapping, especially from 1750 to 1850 as the agricultural revolution was extended northwards. See, for example, B. M. W. Third, 'The Significance of Scottish Estate Plans and Associated Documents', *Scottish Studies* Vol. 1 (1959). In Wales, too, estate maps became common after c.1750, and provide a good coverage of some areas. In the National Library of Wales, for example, the Bute and Dunraven collections contain nearly 300 post-1767 estate maps, mainly relating to Glamorganshire; and the Gogerddan collection contains 160 post-1737 maps of mid and north Cardiganshire.

After 1850 estate maps changed in character. The manuscript surveys of the private practitioners were replaced by the large-scale plans of the Ordnance Survey, on to which base a variety of detail could be added. These plans, although less common in published bibliographies, continue to be an important source of local evidence.

THE CONTENT OF ESTATE MAPS

The contents of estate maps mirror the diversity of the landscape as a whole. For convenience of discussion only we may consider two main groups: the rural estate maps (the most numerous) and the maps depicting industrial subjects—which have been less frequently described.

Rural estate maps

Estate maps paint a uniquely detailed topographical picture, often difficult, sometimes impossible, to obtain elsewhere. The surveyor, in a day of plotting with dividers and quill pen, recorded the countryside more effectively than the lawyer in many bundles of title deeds; his scales—ranging from below 10″ to even 40″ to one mile—permitted the delineation of relatively minor features. Moreover, as M. W. Beresford has demonstrated in several contexts, an estate map not only illuminates the conditions at the date of survey, it looks back to record earlier landscapes the topography of which may now be erased.

The most valuable estate plans—such as that of Laxton (1635) reproduced by C. S. and C. S. Orwin in *The Open Fields* (2nd ed. 1954)—are accompanied by *books of reference*. These give further facts about the parcels of land identified on the map—such as the tenant's name, the acreage, the land use; and with some buildings, the number of rooms or the type of outbuildings. By no means all estate maps are so accompanied. Alternatively, where a book of reference but not the map has survived, it may be possible to reconstruct the latter from field names with the aid of Tithe or Ordnance Survey plans. In other cases, a summary terrier or key to the holdings is provided on the map itself.

An *aggregate* list of the features shown on estate maps is well nigh a complete inventory of the rural landscape, although the local historian must not expect to encounter all, or even a large proportion, in any one map.

The complex layout of the strips and closes in the village fields (they could number several thousand parcels) is precisely set down as F. G. Emmison illustrates in *Some Types of Common-field Parish* (NCSS, 1964); in hilly parishes (for example in downland) strip lynchets may be distinguished; or again parish boundary marks may have been plotted. The maps were also tenurial, recording ownership, tenancy and farm size. They provide an early record of land utilisation in some cases: arable, meadow and pasture, and, occasionally, crops and rotations are identified; wood, marsh, heath and moor, according to locality, may be demarcated; and orchards, gardens, fishponds, vineyards and hopyards help to elaborate our view of the village economy. Parkland was given special attention: woodlands with their ridings and glades, fenced lawns, ornamental gardens and grottoes are depicted; and the plans of landscape gardeners (projected and completed), such as those of Milton Abbas (Dorset) in 1769 and 1776, also reveal the intimate detail of local change.

Village plans included in estate maps record not only the overall layout of the settlement, but the block plans of larger buildings—some at correct scales. Especially on pre-1700 plans, the main buildings may be drawn in elevation or perspective, perhaps furnishing an architectural record of church, manor house, court house, inn, almshouse, barn or school; we may even distinguish roofing materials, of tile or thatch, and discern which windows had glass. Sites of rural industries abound on estate maps; including forges, furnaces and glasshouses; brick and lime kilns; pits for chalk, sand, gravel, stone and marl; tanyards and saltings; and a variety of mills—wind, water and tide, fulling, corn and paper. The minor roads, lanes and droveways, the innumerable bridleways and tracks, toll bars, fords, bridges and ferries were also surveyed in a period when they were often lacking on other classes of maps.

As a source of minor field names, estate maps commend themselves to the philologist and to the economic historian (see, for example, 'Dorset Field Names and the Agricultural Revolution', by Barbara Kerr, *Dorset Natural History and Archaeological Society* Vol. 82 (1961)). Nor should we forget that like Goldsmith's village master—'Lands he could measure, terms and tides presage'—the local surveyor was often an educated man well informed about antiquity as well as the present. Tumuli and other earthworks find a place on estate maps from Elizabethan times onwards, and occasionally a surveyor would record a lost village—as in the case cited by M. W. Beresford in 'Fallowfield, Northumberland: an early cartographic representation of a deserted village', *Medieval Archaeology* Vol. X (1966). Once commissioned, little escaped the sharp eye of the land surveyor.

Estate maps can be minor works of art, and their decorated borders, scales and compass roses, in fresh, bright colours, have merited such terms as 'delicate', 'exquisite' and 'exuberant'. Some surveyors copied the wild flowers, animals, birds and trees of the countryside; others culled their motifs from contemporary books, furniture and architecture, so that we can trace in local cartography the baroque, the rococo, the classical and the romantic; yet others pleased their patrons by heraldry or a large-scale drawing of the manor house. Decoration can inform as well as delight. Style may be a trademark enabling us to identify otherwise anonymous work. Or in a cartouche agricultural practices such as B. R. S. Megaw describes in 'Farm and Fishing Scenes on a Caithness Plan 1772', *Scottish Studies* Vol. VI (1962), may be documented. Few plans can surpass the vivid panorama of rural life portrayed on the map of Laxton (1635), where the surveyor adds to the map pictures of the villagers at work in the fields. 'Most farming operations are portrayed', C. S. Orwin writes, 'ploughing, sowing, harrowing, and harvesting; mowing, haymaking, milking and shepherding . . . The sporting scenes include stag-hunting, hare-hunting, and hawking, and these and the agricultural pictures illustrate both the methods and the costume of the time.' The plan of part of Bowland Forest (Plate 3), although less extensive, likewise brings to life the eighteenth century by means of its realistic drawings of horsemen, hounds and deer, and of the surveyor and his two assistants at work with plane table and chain (Lancashire Record Office, DDX/19/80).

Estate plans of industrial areas

Much of the work of the estate surveyor was related to the countryside. Yet just as we should not ignore the town plans made by estate surveyors (see above), so, too, we should not neglect estate maps which depict industrial subjects, though they have received less limelight than have rural plans. One reason is that most of the published bibliographies of estate maps cover the rural counties of southern England, although industrial maps are fairly numerous in the *Scottish Record Office Descriptive List of Plans*. But there is no doubt that in the coalfield counties, and in the mining districts such as those of Cornwall and Derbyshire, industry will be well represented in local map collections, both amongst estate plans and in the collections of mining surveyors. A *priori* we might expect the need for such plans to be greater, as land values rose with industry, and as disputes over mineral rights led to frequent litigation. Some of our earliest industrial plans, such as those of Cowpen (1598) and Benwell (1637) in Northumberland, reproduced by J. U. Nef, in *The Rise of the British Coal Industry* (1966 ed. Vol. 1), accompanied pleas over the tenant-right to mine coal in the demesne. Later, to avoid ambiguity, landowners had special royalty plans made showing their mineral rights at the surface.

Industrial plans require some classification. An important group relate to *underground* mine working and, apart from those located in estate papers, historians could usefully consult the archives of the National Coal Board. The plans depicting the *surface* evidence of industrial activity are equally numerous, although there are marked gradations in the amount of industrial information they contain. Some are basically rural maps with a light scatter of industry (so characteristic of the coalfield districts before the Railway Age) and either field names, such as 'coal pit field' and 'pit hey', may provide evidence, or the surveyor might write on the map 'coals', 'coal pit drain', 'ironstone' and (more exotic) 'where gold is found'. Many plans, however, were designed *specifically* to show industrial features and will locate sites with greater precision. A 'Map of Land in Orrell', Lancashire, for instance (c.1785) shows the stake of each owner and tenant, disused and active pits, 'soughs', auger holes and drifts (Lancashire Record Office, DDX/233/1). An aggregate list of features on these plans would again be a long one. In mining districts they include lines of seams (long before the official Geological Survey) with the names of those working them, clusters of bell pits, collieries, engine houses and mineral tramways; in textile areas cotton, spinning and carding mills, dyeworks and bleach greens may be depicted; and, in most industrial regions, water-power sites with ponds, dams and leads, something of the detailed topography of communications—canal, road and rail—and, not least, a record of the haphazard scatter of domestic settlement which grew piecemeal with the spread of industry. The cartouches of these plans sometimes picture industrial scenes.

Still more detailed are the large-scale delineations of individual industrial concerns. The 1753 plan of the Darby works at Coalbrookdale, for instance, reproduced in Arthur Raistrick's *Dynasty of Iron Founders* (1953), identified some forty buildings put to various industrial uses—including forges, furnaces, blacksmiths' shops, a moulding house, a stamper mill and a charcoal house; while a detailed 'Map of Land Belonging to the Proprietors of the Parys Mine . . . in Angelsey' (1815) shows intense industrial activity superimposed on a pastoral landscape: not only are shafts and waste heaps located, but much of the supporting paraphernalia — hand and horse whimseys, pumps, precipitation pits, reservoirs, brimstone yards and grounds allotted for copper kilns. In such cases no industrial historian can afford to ignore the evidence of local cartography.

3 Enclosure and tithe maps

Prior to 1850 the enclosure or tithe map may represent the high-water mark in the cartographic documentation of many parishes. Their value is high, not only historically, but also legally as a *terminus ad quem* in many local matters. They are large-scale manuscript plans belonging to the same cartographic family as the estate map; indeed, some surveyors had been engaged on all three types of survey. But while estate plans resulted from the local administration of private property, enclosure and tithe maps were the by-product of legislative activity of a far-reaching character—resulting from either a private enclosure act or the General Enclosure Acts of 1836 and 1845, or from the Tithe Commutation Act of 1836.

Enclosure and tithe maps tend to complement rather than to supplement each other in both date and geographical coverage. While the Parliamentary enclosure surveys are mainly spread out over the century or so after 1750, the tithe maps are concentrated in the mid-nineteenth century. Moreover, those areas richest in enclosure maps are sometimes (but not invariably) correspondingly weak in tithe maps, since at the time of an enclosure act the tithes were usually commuted, removing the need for a full survey by the Tithe Commissioners. Both Gilbert Slater in *The English Peasantry and the Enclosure of Common Fields* (1907), and E. C. K. Gonner in *Common Land and Inclosure* (1912, sec. ed., 1966) had appreciated the consequences of this for the geographical availability of the two sources: Figure 2a, acting as a rough guide to the county percentage of enclosure acts and (for some counties) tithe surveys, is based on their calculations. At the two extremes, Northamptonshire with about half of its area covered by enclosure acts had roughly only a quarter of its area covered by the tithe survey; but Devon and Kent, with virtually no Parliamentary enclosure acts, had an almost complete coverage by tithe awards. This map, however, is inadequate as a detailed local guide: ideally we require a national series of county diagrams showing the availability of both groups of maps at a parish level.

Apart from the still important studies by Gonner and Slater, and the books by Emmison (1966) and West (1962), there are several good introductions to enclosure and tithe evidence—although not dealing with the maps exclusively. *The Parish Chest* (1946), by W. E. Tate, contains concise descriptions of both sources; and, for enclosure, the same author's 'Enclosure Awards and Acts', *History* vol. 51 (1966) and R. A. C. Parker's *Enclosures in the Eighteenth Century* (Historical Association, 1960), provide an excellent background. The two articles on 'The Records of the Tithe Redemption Commission', by the Secretary of the Commission, in the *Journal of the Society of Archivists* vol. 1 (1956) and on 'The Tithe Surveys of the Mid-Nineteenth Century', by H. C. Prince, *The Agricultural History Review* vol. VII (1959) similarly provide authoritative accounts. Many studies by historians and geographers are indebted to the source, but no local historian should fail to examine some of the composite parish maps, based on estate, enclosure and tithe plans, which appear in the recently published volumes for Oxfordshire and Wiltshire of *The Victoria History of the Counties of England.*

The listing of English enclosure awards and acts is well advanced. Pioneer lists were compiled by Slater (as Appendix B to his book), but today, we are deeply indebted to the county handlists prepared by W. E. Tate, usually published in the local historical society *Proceedings* or *Transactions* (although not all specify the existence of maps). W. H. Chaloner has listed these in his 'Bibliography of Recent Work on Enclosure, the Open Fields, and related topics', *The Agricultural History Review*, vol. II (1954); and another useful list, arranged by counties, appears in John West's *Village Records.* Recently, Mr. Tate has charted his own progress, with an index map (Figure 2c) in 'A Domesday of English Enclosure Acts and Awards', *The Amateur Historian* vol. 5 (1963) and this represents the present position; when complete his work will provide a full index of English Parliamentary enclosures from 1603 to 1914.

Two copies of the enclosure award and map were made, the place of deposit of which is sometimes specified by the Act. Generally speaking, however, one copy remained with the enclosed parish, and the other was put on official deposit with the Clerk of the Peace. Today, both sets of plans may have found their way into the County Record Office, although some copies are elsewhere, notably in the Public Record Office, which is particularly rich in enclosure plans of both Crown and private estates. Many County Record Offices have prepared lists of their enclosure documents: some are mimeographed; some are separate publications as Peter Walne's *A Catalogue of Inclosure Maps in the Berkshire Record Office* (1954), or a *Handlist of Inclosure Acts and Awards relating to the County of Oxford* (Oxford County Council, 1963); some are in map catalogues such as those for Essex and Sussex; some form sections in general guides as in the *Index to the Dorset County Records*

(1938), or the Guide to the Hertfordshire Record Office Part I (1961); and some are listed by parishes as in the Guide to the Parish Records of the City of Bristol and the County of Gloucester (Bristol and Glos. Arch. Soc., 1963). Many of these publications are listed in Philip Hepworth's useful Archives and Manuscripts in Libraries (Library Association, sec. ed., 1964). Other handlists, as the List of West Riding Enclosure Awards, have been compiled for the National Register of Archives. All should be consulted for additions to earlier lists by W. E. Tate.

An introduction to the Welsh enclosure evidence will be found in Agriculture in Wales during the Napoleonic Wars (1963) by David Thomas; and, for its area, A. H. Dodd's The Industrial Revolution in North Wales (1933, sec. ed., 1951) is particularly useful. A chronological list of private enclosure acts was incorporated by Ivor Bowen in The Great Inclosures of Common Lands in Wales (1914) and this can be supplemented by T. I. Jeffreys Jones's Acts of Parliament Concerning Wales 1714-1901 (Cardiff, 1959). The Guide to the Caernarvonshire Record Office (C.C.R.O., 1952) includes a list of enclosure awards and maps, but, in general, the Welsh counties lag behind in this field of cartographic bibliography. Some of the maps and awards are deposited in the County Record Offices, but the National Library of Wales houses material relating to Montgomeryshire (47 awards and maps) and Cardiganshire (15 awards and maps).

Scotland is a different case. Although an analogous process of enclosure resulted in numerous large-scale plans (often to depict an estate before and after improvement) these were not a by-product of Parliamentary legislation, but were executed for independent landlords. The resulting maps, although they were often uniformly prepared for one estate, vary considerably in design and content and have been classified as estate plans (see above).

The bibliography of Tithe Maps is an easier task because of their unity of date and administrative origin. We are also fortunate insofar as the Return of all Tithes Commuted and Apportioned under the Acts for Commutation of Tithes (British Sessional Papers, House of Commons, 1887, vol. LXIV pp. 239-533), is in effect a complete list of all districts (parish, township or smaller unit) for which tithe apportionments and maps exist, although it is itself concerned with income rather than acreage. The tithe documents were prepared in triplicate. One copy remained in the custody of the Tithe Redemption Commission,[1] but these originals, after microfilming, have been transferred to the Public Record Office.[2] A second copy was deposited in the Diocesan records, and a third with the incumbent of the parish. The first copies survive complete and provide a central national archive, but the survival of the second and third (especially the parish copies) is more patchy. However, these latter are convenient for local consultation and will often be

[1] Now Tithe Redemption Office, East Block, Barrington Road, Worthing, Sussex.
[2] At present stored at Ashridge, Berkhampstead, Herts.

31

found in the County Record Offices—where they have been catalogued in some of the *Guides* referred to above—while others remain in Diocesan Record Offices. An almost complete set of tithe maps for the parishes of Wales is in the National Library of Wales. The tithe survey did not extend to Scotland.

ENCLOSURE MAPS

The enclosure movement which culminated in the Georgian era had antecedents extending back to the medieval period, and its nature is well illustrated in a local study (with maps) by Arthur G. Ruston and Denis Witney, *Hooton Pagnell: The Agricultural Evolution of a Yorkshire Village* (1934). Many 'estate' maps in fact accompanied enclosures privately agreed between landlords or groups of tenants without an Act of Parliament, and such plans are, of course, essential to the theme of the enclosure historian. With the era of Parliamentary enclosure, however, we encounter a cartographic source of much greater magnitude. For England, alone, W. E. Tate has calculated that the Acts related to lands in roughly 5,000 ancient parishes, and parts of at least several hundred Welsh parishes must have been affected.

There were two major enclosure documents, the award — the written record of the Commissioner's decisions about a variety of topographical, economic and tenurial matters of interest to the historian—and, especially after about 1770, a large-scale plan to identify the lands in question. Either one or both may have survived but these two parts of the document were designed to be used together, and the value of the maps would be considerably lessened if used in isolation. The maps, however, were far from stereotyped. They range from the detailed delineation of a whole parish to the barest sketch of a few acres of waste; and, especially before 1800, there was much variety in scale and cartographic style. We should also distinguish between the two major groups of enclosures these maps illustrate—first, the common arable fields and common meadows; secondly, the other commons such as heath, forest, marsh and moorland.

Maps of arable fields and meadows

For the broad segment of lowland England identified by Slater and Gonner (Figure 2a), the maps made in connection with the re-allotment of arable and meadow strips, and their eventual replacement by the modern hedged fields, are a major parish record—although, of course, enclosure often affected the other types of common within this zone (see, for example, Joan Thirsk, *English Peasant Farming* (1957) where enclosures in the Lincolnshire clayland, fenland, marshland and upland heath are described). The enclosure plans attached to the Award usually depicted the new landscape after the Commissioners had done their work, and their use in a regional study is admirably demonstrated by Alan Harris, *The Rural Landscape of the East Riding of Yorkshire 1700-1850* (1961). Although the maps are sometimes sparse in topographical

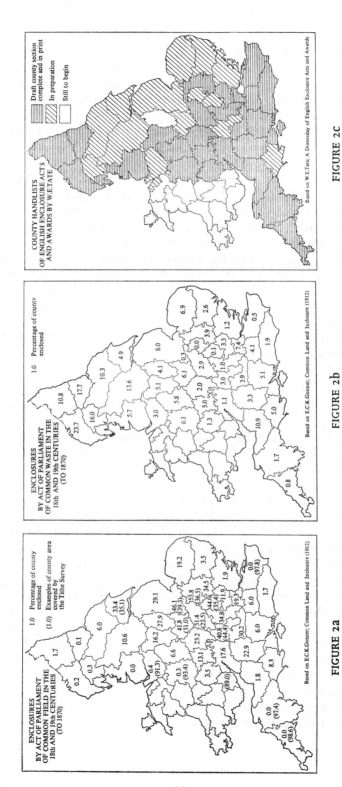

COUNTY HANDLISTS
OF ENGLISH ENCLOSURE ACTS
AND AWARDS BY W.E.TATE

Draft county section
complete and in print

In preparation

Still to begin

Based on W.E.Tate; A Domesday of English Enclosure Acts and Awards

FIGURE 2c

ENCLOSURES
BY ACT OF PARLIAMENT
OF COMMON WASTE IN THE
18th AND 19th CENTURIES
(TO 1870)

1.0 Percentage of county
     enclosed

Based on E.C.K.Gonner; Common Land and Inclosure (1912)

FIGURE 2b

ENCLOSURES
BY ACT OF PARLIAMENT
OF COMMON FIELD IN THE
18th AND 19th CENTURIES
(TO 1870)

1.0 Percentage of county
     enclosed

(1.0) Examples of county area
       covered by
       the Tithe Survey

Based on E.C.K.Gonner; Common Land and Inclosure (1912)

FIGURE 2a

33

detail, many are comparable with the best estate maps, and include the 'ancient' enclosures and the village itself, as well as the lands which were currently subject to enclosure. Not only do they provide an historical record including settlements, boundaries, landownership, tenures, field names and rural industries; but on subjects including the course and breadth of public and private roads, the line of footpaths and rights of way, the responsibility for drains, certain mineral rights, and the territorial endowments of schools and charities, they may be an ultimate legal authority.

The so-called draft enclosure plans, which became more common after 1830, may also be extant—although many are now lost. Insofar as they represent a preliminary survey of the township in its open state, they are especially valuable in depicting the *pre-enclosure parish*—the lands still sub-divided in strips (see F. G. Emmison, *Some Types of Common-Field Parish*). Sometimes, too, as in the Cambridgeshire village of Barton, 1840, we glimpse the surveyor's plan at a slightly later phase, showing both the exist-ing ownership, and the preliminary proposals for enclosure allotment super-imposed on the older field pattern. Another duty of the enclosure surveyor was to investigate the evidence of old surveys, so that a copy of a much earlier estate map (perhaps the only extant copy) may be in the company of the other enclosure documents.

Maps of waste lands

Outside central England, especially in the nineteenth century when the movement gathered momentum, the commonest type of enclosure map was one accompanying an act for the enclosure of common waste lands (Figure 2b). The importance of such evidence for a local study in the Highland Zone is illustrated by J. G. Thomas, 'The distribution of the commons in part of Arwystli at the time of enclosure' *Montgomeryshire Collections* vol. 54 (1955). In Arwystli, an enclosure of 1826 dealt with an upland moor, and the map and award enabled not only the old enclosures, the common waste and illegal encroachments to be reconstructed, but also the new land units and settlements created by the act. In other areas, where agricultural and indus-trial colonisation went hand in hand, the maps have a double interest. In the North Pennines, for example, as A. E. Smailes shows in *North England* (1960), the Parliamentary enclosure movement coincided with a spread of mining and resulted in the settlement and division of large areas of moorland. The carto-graphic evidence accompanying the transformation of lowlying 'wastes' is also voluminous. At one time or another during the Agricultural Revolution the reclamation of parts of areas such as the Fens, the Isle of Axholme, the Somerset Levels, the Lancashire mosses, numerous marshes around the coasts of Britain, and former areas of Royal Forest (for the last-named see the Forestry Commission maps in the Public Record Office) had all come within the ambit of the enclosure surveyor.

The tithe surveys have been justly described as the land surveyor's most valuable legacy to the local historian. They extended to some 11,800 parishes or townships in England and Wales, covering roughly 79 per cent of the area. The maps furnished the first large-scale survey of a large part of the country, pre-dating the 6" and 25" maps of the Ordnance Survey by nearly a generation in some areas. Indeed, the Tithe Commissioners conceived their task as a national *cadastre*—'a General Survey and Register of Real Property' —comparable to Domesday Book. Unlike the attenuated and patchy nature of the estate and enclosure evidence for many regions, most of the tithe maps were made from 1836 to 1841, the rest by 1851, apart from the altered apportionments and maps made following radical changes such as those due to railway or suburban development.

The two major documents are the plans and the written apportionments, which were again designed to be used together, because the plans themselves often give only limited information. As a set, however, the plans fell short of the original blueprint for a uniform series. Their size was partly proportional to that of the parishes, so that they range from one to over a hundred square feet. The differences were accentuated by scales which varied from one to twelve chains to the inch—although maps on the three, four and six chains scale[1] comprise about three-quarters of the total. They also vary considerably in accuracy depending on the skill of the many hundreds of local surveyors employed on the task. The first specification for the mapping, drawn up by Lieutenant R. K. Dawson of the Ordnance Survey (who was an Assistant Tithe Commissioner), proved to be over-ambitious; in 183ʒ amending legislation had to be passed to permit the making of less accurate maps, often on a smaller scale. However, the Tithe Commissioners refused their seal to inferior plans, and only about 1,900, roughly a sixth of the total, were eventually sealed as first class maps. The remainder were a mixed bag: some were original surveys; others were copies of slightly earlier maps; some made elaborate use of colours to distinguish different properties, tithe-free areas, or land use; but a number were little more than topographical sketches, and of no cadastral value as some of the witnesses before a Royal Commission on the Ordnance Survey (B.P.P. 1857-8, xix, 615-6) were to point out.

The written tithe documents follow a more rigid formula. For each numbered parcel or building on the map the apportionment furnishes standard information as to the owner, the occupier, the name and description of the lands and premises, the state of cultivation (arable, pasture, etc., although the accuracy of this information is sometimes suspect), the acreage of each parcel, and the rental apportioned on the land within the titheable area. The total result is an immensely detailed—almost exhaustive—local inventory, including details of settlement (many maps show dwellings in red, other buildings

[1] i.e. approximately 26·6", 20" and 13·3" to one mile.

in grey, and sometimes larger edifices such as churches or windmills in elevation), parish, field and farm boundaries, land use, field-names, the extent of common, heaths and greens, the progress of enclosure (where this was not accomplished the tithe map may be a common-field strip map), and the intricacies of tenure. Moreover, these aspects are depicted at a critical time in their history, on the eve of the era of 'High Farming' and before the Great Agricultural Depression.

Quite naturally the tithe documents have been used extensively in the reconstruction of rural conditions. To quote but one instance, after pioneer studies, such as that by E. C. Willatts, 'Changes in land utilization in the South West of the London Basin', Geographical Journal vol. 82 (1933), they were widely employed in the historical sections of the County Reports of the Land Utilisation Survey of Britain, edited by the late Sir Dudley Stamp. But their importance for the study of urban and industrial areas must not be overlooked. The work of the Tithe Commissioners extended to many towns, for instance Leeds, which was surveyed separately in 1847 at a scale of 27 inches to a mile; in addition smaller country towns were sometimes inset into the maps at a larger scale. Not least, in many industrial areas, tithe maps record conditions towards the end of the early railway age. They may be the first detailed parish maps to show the impact of industry and railway development (Plate 4).

THE EVALUATION OF ESTATE, ENCLOSURE AND TITHE MAPS

In considering the principles by which their reliability may be assessed, estate, enclosure and tithe maps may be conveniently grouped together. Both the symptoms and the causes of their inaccuracies are numerous; and their interpretation, despite an apparent graphic simplicity, may bristle with difficulty. Ambiguity is a recurrent problem because varying symbols may be used by different surveyors to depict the same feature, or conversely, as A. R. H. Baker points out in 'Some Kentish Estate Maps and a note on their portrayal of Field Boundaries', Archaeologia Cantiana, vol. 77 (1962), the same symbol may be used to depict different features, and the intention is not always clear. Terminology may also be inconsistent, as in the designation of different categories of grassland; and in Wales, for example, the 'common and waste' of the private surveyors became 'rough pasture' on the Ordnance Survey plans. As a result, as J. T. Coppock shows in 'Changes in Farm and Field Boundaries in the Nineteenth Century', The Amateur Historian vol. 3 (1956-58), comparisons may be difficult to effect. In any case all surveyors were obviously not equally competent. On the one hand, M. W. Beresford concluded that Ralph Agas' plan of Toddington (1581), was ' . . . so carefully drawn and on such a large scale that Agas must have made an instrumental survey; even the trees and hedges are shown in their real position . . . ', but, on the other hand, F. G. Emmison points to seventeenth- and eighteenth-century estate plans of Essex which 'bear little resemblance to the property

36

described'. Although large-scale manuscript maps in general become more accurate over the period 1550-1850, the mathematical revolution in surveying was not diffused with equal speed and there was much variety in local practice. Even those maps intended to have legal authority, such as the tithe and enclosure surveys, did not attain uniform quality. Accordingly, it may be helpful for the local historian to bear in mind three considerations which seem to be fundamental.

(i) *First*, it is a golden rule that maps should not be used in isolation but to complement other classes of evidence. Cognate documentary sources are needed to throw light on the accuracy of maps, their purpose, the methods by which they were made, and to establish how much of the cartographer's information is unique, and how much is merely a repetition of what can be obtained elsewhere. Maps seldom elucidate the *whole* story required by the historian. Local manuscript maps are only one link in a chain of evidence including documents, aerial photographs and above all field study; or a map may only pose a question whose solution lies in other sources. Furthermore, estate, enclosure and tithe maps are only the graphic part of a larger manuscript survey, and the accompanying books of reference, awards and schedules are a necessary key to the data on the map. In the case of tithe surveys, the tithe files (see E. A. Cox and B. R. Dittmer, 'The Tithe Files of the Mid-Nineteenth Century' *The Agricultural History Review* vol. XIII (1965) may also be needed to complete the picture.

But evidence divorced from the maps, and of a quite random nature, can also assist historical interpretation. A single example must suffice. Even if we were unaware that the Tithe Commissioners had refused to grant their seal to many maps, the fact that Colonel Thomas Colby, Director of the Ordnance Survey, had written (in a personal letter) of 'poor Dawson's complete failure in the tithe commutation business', might put us on our guard. A further search in the Parliamentary Papers would uncover the objection of many landowners to the mapping of extensive tithe-free lands at their expense, and the fact that they had canvassed a cheaper method of compilation from existing parochial and township maps (quoted by R. A. Skelton in 'Maps and the Local Historian', *Middlesex Local History Council Bulletin*, No. 11 (1961). The sources which throw new light on early maps are as diverse as the character of the maps themselves, but, to date, researchers have only skimmed this evidence.

(ii) *Secondly*, the historian should always ask how the map was made—the crucial factor in its reliability. Only then can we say how much of its data resulted from genuine field work, how much from cursory examination, from the oral testimony of others, or from the inspection of other estate documents. And if the map was based on field survey, the question of technique becomes important. What instruments did the surveyor use and how reliable were they? Was the plan based on triangulation or some more primi-

37

tive system? Was the treatment of some parts of the survey more superficial than others? The normal practice of surveyors in making several contemporary copies of their plans (albeit for legitimate purposes) can introduce errors in the transcription of names, figures and outlines; and, as this was a continuous process it may be cumulative, and the correct date of *survey*, as opposed to that of drawing, must always be established. Extra 'unofficial' copies were made even of tithe and enclosure maps and where several drafts have survived we must decide which is the most accurate.

The optimum guide to a surveyor's methods lies, of course, in his professional papers. The Fairbank collection in Sheffield City Library and the papers of James Fish of Warwick, junior, in the Warwickshire County Record Office, include working notebooks from which the survey lines for estate maps were plotted (they sometimes contain more detail than the final version), rough drafts of plans, accounts and correspondence. They effectively place us at the side of the early surveyor in both the field and the office, and the stages and timetable of his activities — which could sometimes be protracted — become meaningful; indeed, they provide the only safe credentials to a surveyor's practice. The new light which such documentation can throw on the map-making process is demonstrated by Peter L. Hull in an interesting background article 'Some Bedfordshire Surveyors of the Eighteenth Century' *Journal of the Society of Archivists* vol. 1 (1957).

Failing this (and surveyors' papers are by no means common) it is helpful to consider a map in the light of the contemporary surveying manuals which, from the sixteenth century onwards, were used for professional instruction. The developments they embody have recently been summarised by A. W. Richeson, *English Land Measuring to 1800: Instruments and Practice* (Massachussetts Institute of Technology, 1966). This helps us to infer the technical competence of a surveyor at a particular date, and the theoretical (if not the practical) limitations to the accuracy of his maps. Similarly, no historian who intends to use the tithe maps should neglect to peruse the *Copy of Papers Respecting the Proposed Survey of Lands under the Tithe Act* (British Sessional Papers, House of Commons, 1837, vol. XLI p. 383 *et seq.*) and the other Parliamentary papers which set down Dawson's specifications for the survey, as well as the instructions to tithe surveyors reproduced in contemporary legal manuals such as Leonard Shelford's *The Acts for the Commutation of Tithes in England and Wales* (3rd ed., 1842). These are the terms of reference in the light of which the evidence of the maps must be assessed. Only then, for example, can we appreciate why the information about rights of way on Tithe maps is seldom precise and often ambiguous; for this was no concern of the Commissioners.

(iii) Thirdly, the historian should search for methods of testing the accuracy of his maps. Most maps can be subjected to simple tests to check their scale, distortion and orientation against accurate modern plans, although

38

we should remember that these mathematical properties may be inconsistent within one map. Palaeography or cartographic style may help to establish the date and authorship of a map if this is in question; at the same time, we should guard against seduction by the neat and artistic map; the most crudely drafted plans are not necessarily those of least historical value. The internal consistency of the surveyor's arithmetic can also be checked perhaps to reveal minor errors, such as the discrepancies between terrier and map which C. S. Orwin found in the survey of Laxton, but sometimes, as in a seventeenth-century survey of Yorkshire — where a Kentish surveyor was still using Kentish units of land measurement—to unearth a more unusual type of deviation (see T. S. Willan and E. W. Crossley (eds.) *Three Seventeenth Century Yorkshire Surveys* (Yorks. Arch. Soc. Record Series vol. civ (1941)). On tithe maps, too, clerical errors are revealed by checking parish and diocesan copies against the Tithe Redemption copies; and, even greater discrepancies may occur between the information recorded on the map, and in the apportionment (they can be of different dates, just as the enclosure map can precede the award by a number of years).

The internal content of all local manuscript maps should, as a matter of routine, be compared with other topographical sources. The first editions of the 6″ and 25″ maps of the Ordnance Survey provide an authority from which to work back; and on good estate maps inaccuracies in shapes and areas may be negligible—as E. Straker found with the Sussex maps accompanying the Buckhurst terrier (see p. 24). Estate plans may also be compared with tithe plans; with other estate plans (especially where there is a sequence of maps for one property); with the maps accompanying sale catalogues—a neglected source of cartographic evidence; with the surveyor's drawings for the First Edition of the Ordnance Survey one-inch map (at scales of 2″ to 6″ to one mile and showing field boundaries); and with county maps (see pp. 63-76). When comparing such maps, to assess either accuracy or change, it may be useful to re-plot the relevant information on a common scale, or to adjust the scales by photographic means, to help in the process of sifting *actual* change from cartographic ambiguity. Non-cartographic sources, especially estate documents containing detailed topographical information, may also be used for authenticating the evidence on a map; and, finally, cartographic detail may be compared with either aerial photographs or, by means of photostat copies, with the ground itself. No standard set of tests is appropriate to all maps, yet some sort of evaluation must necessarily be made of every single map before the historian can use its evidence with confidence.

4 Maps of communications

Routeways have been depicted on maps from the earliest times and are an integral feature of most of the maps described elsewhere in the *Guide*. The present section is therefore confined to *specialist* maps of communications[1] designed to show either the line of a route and its adjacent topography or the network of communications. Little has been written on the history of such maps of communications, although much can be gleaned from the voluminous literature of the history of British transport as a whole (e.g. W. T. Jackman's *The Development of Transportation in Modern England* (1916, 2nd ed. 1966)). Each of the major developments in communications has left its imprint in the maps of Britain at both national and local levels, and the map-maker was involved in each stage of evolution of most transport projects. Maps served as a regular adjunct to the propaganda for a new scheme; the engineering work required a detailed survey; and new roads, canals and railways called for revision of existing maps, as well as giving scope for special maps to meet the needs of transport users. Some maps of communications are thus the original work of highly skilled surveyors, but others the edited versions of commercial map publishing houses: in evaluating them we must bear this in mind. All have a dual interest—not only for the history of transport and related subjects, but also for many branches of purely local history.

BIBLIOGRAPHIES OF MAPS OF COMMUNICATIONS

Transport maps are so diverse in character, and so scattered in archives and libraries, that no single bibliography of any area in Britain has yet been compiled. On the other hand, representative examples of most categories of transport maps will be found in some of the general catalogues already noted for estate, enclosure and town plans. Insofar as many maps of communications have remained in manuscript, the class as a whole has offered less scope for

---

[1] Strictly interpreted the scope of 'Maps of Communications' would extend, *inter alia*, to maps showing telegraphs, telephones and air transport; they have been excluded as being of only marginal interest to local historians.

detailed carto-bibliographical analysis than either town plans or county maps. The main exception is the printed maps of roads, published in books and atlases from the seventeenth century onwards, and for which the pioneer studies of H. G. Fordham, although now in need of revision, are still indispensable: his *The Road-Books and Itineraries of Great Britain, 1570-1850* (1924) is especially useful, but other details can be culled from his 'The Road-Books of Wales with a Catalogue, 1775-1850', *Archaeologia Cambrensis* vol. 82 (1927). Thomas Chubb's *The Printed Maps in the Atlases of Great Britain and Ireland A Bibliography, 1579-1870* (1927) is also useful for this purpose.

Those record offices which have particularly good collections of transport maps include, for the country as a whole, the House of Lords Record Office, a premier archive of transport plans, the documentary context of which is discussed by Maurice Bond in 'Materials for Transport History amongst the Records of Parliament', *The Journal of Transport History*, Vol. 4 (1959-60). All schemes for river, canal, road and railway improvement required a private Act of Parliament, and after 1792 the promoters had to submit an exact plan of the land they intended to traverse and a book of reference giving details of the owners and occupiers of each parcel of land so crossed. After 1807 the plans were at scales of not less than 4" to a mile. This legislation has resulted in several substantial categories of Parliamentary plans classified under bridges, ferries, roads, subways and tunnels; railways, omnibuses, tramways and trolley vehicles; and canals, rivers and navigations, but many of which have a basically similar format. The same legislation required duplicate plans to be lodged with the Clerk of the Peace, and these copies are preserved in the County Record Office, where they may be listed in map catalogues as for Essex and for West Sussex (where full details of maps of all public schemes are included in *A Catalogue of Sussex Estate Maps, West Sussex Inclosure Maps, West Sussex Deposited Plans, Miscellaneous and Printed Sussex Maps*, Sussex Record Society Vol. 66 (1968), edited by F. W. Steer), in consolidated sections of publications such as the *Guide to the Flintshire Record Office* (1955) and the *Guide to the Nottinghamshire County Records Office* (1963), or on separate mimeographed lists such as the Worcestershire Record Office's 'Handlist of plans, sections, books of reference and other documents deposited with the Clerk of the County Council . . . pertaining to public schemes' (1955). Railways plans have been listed for over twenty counties either in such works or separately as in Cheshire County Council's *Alphabetical List of Deposited Plans at the County Record Office . . . regarding Railways . . .* (1953) and *A Handlist of Plans Sections and Books of Reference for the Proposed Railways in Oxfordshire 1825-1936* (1964), issued by the Oxfordshire County Council.

The British Transport Historical Records in London[1] and Edinburgh[2] also

[1] 66 Porchester Road, Paddington, London W.2.
[2] 23 Waterloo Place, Edinburgh.

maintain specialist collections of plans derived from the papers of the former transport operators. The emphasis is on railway material, and a useful introduction to their scope will be found in L. C. Johnson's 'Historical Records of the British Transport Commission', *The Journal of Transport History*, Vol. 1 (1953-54). In addition, the York depository of the British Railways Board contains a group of railway maps and plans, noted by E. H. Fowkes in *Railway History and the Local Historian* (East Yorkshire Local History Society, 1963). A less well-used archive is probably that of the General Post Office[1], containing a number of nineteenth-century maps showing the routes of mail coaches, horse posts and foot posts, together with numerous local sketch maps amongst the reports to the Postmaster General from District Surveyors in the period 1791-1843.

Many canal and railway schemes were so much in the public eye that, to satisfy the demand for information, engraved or lithographed plans had to be prepared. The Map Room of the British Museum has a large collection of this printed material; and, in the *Catalogue of Printed Maps . . .* (1967) the entries are consolidated under *England Canal Maps* (there is also a separate typescript 'List of Canal Maps' on the reference shelves); *Scotland Canal Maps*; *England Railway, Maps*; *England Road Atlases*—and so on. The Public Record Office also has a worthwhile collection of maps of communications in various departmental classes, listed in *Maps and Plans in the Public Record Office* 1 . . . (1967), and with railway material noted by D. B. Wardle, in 'Sources for the History of Railways at the Public Record Office', *The Journal of Transport History*, Vol. 2 (1955-56). In Scotland, transport plans form a substantial group in the Scottish Record Office, and an outline bibliography of the printed maps of roads, canals and railways is incorporated in *The Early Maps of Scotland* (1936).

MAPS OF ROADS

Maps of roads are amongst the most ancient known to historians of cartography. The Peutinger Table, dating to the second half of the fourth century A.D., was a road map of the Roman Empire; and although part of the section relating to Britain was missing, it is reconstructed in Conrad Miller, *Die Peutingersche Tafel* (Ravensburg, 1888; reprint, Stuttgart, 1962). On the few medieval maps of Great Britain roads were also prominently depicted and, indeed, were one of their main *raison d'être*. The Mathew Paris Map (c. 1250) reproduced in *Four Maps of Great Britain designed by Mathew Paris* (British Museum, 1928), and discussed by J. B. Mitchell in *The Geographical Journal* Vol. 81 (1933), was constructed round an itinerary from Newcastle to Dover via London; later, the most outstanding feature of the more sophisticated Gough Map was the detailed representation, with

[1] Post Office Records, Headquarters Building, St. Martins-le-Grand, London, E.C.1.

inter-town distances, of the fourteenth-century road system (see E. J. S. Parsons, *The Map of Great Britain c. A.D. 1360, Known as the Gough Map* (Bodleian Library and R.G.S., 1958). Even on the Hereford *mappa mundi*, as G. R. Crone has recently demonstrated in 'New Light on the Hereford Map', *The Geographical Journal*, Vol. 131 (1965), a number of thirteenth-century trade and pilgrim routes were added to a primarily religious and mythological representation of the world.

The best account of the successive attempts in the modern period to furnish the traveller with adequate information (cartographic and otherwise) about roads is still H. G. Fordham's *Notes on British Itineraries and road books* (1912). Road books developed from pilgrim guides, becoming common by the end of the Middle Ages, and continued in estimates of distances along main roads made by Tudor topographers and chroniclers such as John Leland, Raphael Holinshed, John Stow and William Smith. But the graphic delineation of roads was curiously neglected. On the first county maps of Christopher Saxton (see p. 67), roads were excluded from the design, and although John Norden sought to remedy this omission in a handful of his county surveys, and invented the (still serviceable) triangular table of distances between towns for his *England: An Intended Guyde for English Travailers* (1625) the age of the specialised road map lay in the future.

It arrived in 1675 with the publication of John Ogilby's *Britannia*, a road book consisting of one hundred plates, each containing six or seven strip maps showing the route of a road. This work (with some of its successors) is described by H. G. Fordham, 'John Ogilby (1600-1676) His *Britannia* and the British Itineraries of the eighteenth century', *The Library* 4th Series, Vol. 6 (1925), and was published in facsimile by Alexander Duckham & Co. Ltd. in 1939. *Britannia* contained the first measured maps of the main roads of England and Wales; it also introduced the statute mile to English printed maps, helped to popularise the scale of one inch to one mile, and became the model for a *genre* of road maps not entirely obsolete today. Its format was even reflected in local manuscript maps such as a series of strip maps (c. 1684) showing the main road northwards through Lancashire (Lancashire Record Office, DDX 194).

Ogilby's roads depict much that is of local topographical interest—see for instance J. B. Harley, 'Ogilby and Collins: Cheshire by Road and Sea', *Cheshire Round*, Vol. 1 no. 7 (1967)—but the particular distinction between fenced and unfenced roads has enabled historians ranging from T. B. Macaulay to E. C. K. Gonner to estimate regional variations in the proportion of open and enclosed land.

In the first half of the eighteenth century Ogilby had several imitators such as Thomas Gardner, John Senex and Emanuel Bowen, but their strip maps were mainly reduced copies of *Britannia*, embodying minor revision. Not until the late-eighteenth century did the improvement of the road system,

43

and especially in turnpiking, stimulate a demand for the production of entirely new road books. These included works by Daniel Paterson, John Owen, Edward Mogg, John Cary, and Laurie and Whittle, and for Scotland by George Taylor and Andrew Skinner. Here again H. G. Fordham's studies of *John Cary Engraver, Map, Chart and Print-Seller and Globe Maker 1754 to 1835* (1925) and 'Daniel Paterson, His Maps and Itineraries, 1738-1825', *The Library*, Vol. 7 (1926) are an indispensable guide to both methods of compilation and the dating of various editions.

Cary's information on roads may be viewed with above-average confidence. The data were derived 'From an Actual Admeasurement . . . Made by Command of His Majesty's Postmaster General, for Official Purposes', and covering some nine thousand miles; moreover, many editions of the road-books and county maps which incorporated these data appear to have undergone some revision. Cary's work also illustrates that not all road books consisted of strip maps; some, although containing small-scale county maps as a key to the roads covered, were essentially tables of the distances between places along the roads, with notes on objects of interest. The road books of Paterson also reflect this distinction: *Paterson's British Itinerary* (first edition, 1785), for instance, adopted the format of Ogilby, but *A New and Accurate Description of the Direct and Principal Cross Roads in Great Britain* (first edition, 1771) merely tabulated the information.

Throughout the nineteenth century road books and road maps were published in great numbers. What Cary's maps had been for the heyday of the stage coach, those of other firms such as George Philip & Son and George Washington, Bacon and Co. were to become for the pioneer days of the bicycle and the motor car. A growing number of tourists fostered a whole range of specialised maps, some of which, for coastal resorts, show and name hotels, lending libraries and other 'attractions'. By 1900, of course, all such maps were either reduced or 'improved' from the Ordnance Survey.

From the eighteenth century onwards the historian can also consult the various plans which were the everyday by-product of road improvement, including those where a private act of Parliament was involved. They vary considerably in purpose, scale and detail. An important group, associated with the diversion and closure of highways, bridleways or footways, are especially numerous for the Georgian period of estate improvement. After 1773, the Quarter Sessions had the authority to confirm these changes and the enrolled documents, including a map, are now in the County Record Office. They may show both the old roads to be diverted and the new roads, together with the area of park or estate involved (Plate 5), and including details of field names, buildings and ownership. After c. 1800 these plans are generally more accurate and detailed, and are frequently coloured.

The turnpike trust documents are also available for the period c. 1700 to c. 1875, with plans common from 1792 onwards. Plans of intended turnpikes, many of which never come to fruition, had to be deposited; improvements to existing turnpikes had to be mapped; and, finally, surveys of disturnpiked roads were sometimes produced. Turnpike plans may present only a bare sketch of the route, but at best may be large-scale strip maps of the road and immediately adjacent areas, often in the form of a roll, and incorporating buildings, field names, owners and occupiers; occasionally the detailed field books for these surveys may have survived as well as sections of roads and separate plans of features such as toll houses and bridges. Bridges were also the object of a separate trust on occasions, the records of which may contain cartographic material—see Edith S. Scroggs 'The Records of Rochester Bridge . . . ', Archives Vol. 2 (1954). When the responsibility for roads passed to the Local Authority in the second half of the nineteenth century, the cartographic record was still maintained in a sequence of engineering plans and sections.

RIVER NAVIGATION AND CANAL MAPS

The best introduction to the maps and plans connected with navigable rivers and canals is the regional histories of British canals edited by Charles Hadfield, including volumes on the East Midlands, South Wales and the Border, the West Midlands, South West England and Southern England, in which every proposed canal (and many river navigations) are separately discussed.

River Navigation Plans

A few plans made in connection with river navigation survive from the sixteenth century onwards. An unusually detailed map, at a scale of c. 9 inches to one mile, showing the navigation of the River Lea in a long strip format, and made some time after its improvement in 1571, is described by G. B. G. Bull, 'Elizabethan Maps of the Lower Lea Valley', *The Geographical Journal* Vol. 124 (1958). Yet such improvement did not gather pace until after the Restoration, and river navigation plans are not numerous until the eighteenth century. T. S. Willan's *River Navigation in England 1600-1750* (1936), sets these plans in their historical context, the chapter on 'Engineers and engineering' being especially pertinent as background to their surveying. Similar ground is usefully trodden by A. W. Skempton in 'The Engineers of the English River Navigations, 1620-1760', *Transactions of the Newcomen Society* Vol. 29 (1958), which includes a list of the principal navigations and biographical notes on the main engineers. Armed thus with Hadfield and with names of engineers and navigations it should not be difficult to locate the plans in repositories already mentioned.

These maps vary in usefulness. Small-scale maps designed to illustrate the general line of a navigation are of little value for detailed topographical research. On the other hand many early river surveys incorporated original work lacking in contemporary maps: in 1697, for instance, Ralph Thoresby noted in his diary how John Hadley, the engineer of the Aire and Calder navigation, had ' . . . followed the windings of the river and measured it with his surveying wheel', a technique which was only exceptionally undertaken for the county maps of the day (see pp. 68-9). By the late-eighteenth century, when civil engineering had become a distinctive profession, men such as Brindley, Smeaton and Rennie produced accurate large-scale plans of their undertakings. The plan for the proposed Chelmer and Blackwater Navigation, 1792-94, for instance, surveyed under the direction of Rennie, was at a scale of 6·6 inches to one mile, and showed considerable detail up to one mile on each side of the river and its proposed new cuts (Essex Record Office Q/RUm 1/1, 1/2). Even relatively limited improvements such as works on individual locks and weirs were accompanied by a detailed plan.

Where river improvement was concerned with tidal water, the distinction between engineering plan and marine chart (see pp. 51-62) was often blurred. The cartographic record for such estuarine areas is particularly full as is illustrated by E. A. G. Clark's study of *The Ports of the Exe Estuary 1660-1860* (1960), or by the plans connected with the navigation and drainage of the Great Ouse in the Kings Lynn area (see Edward Lynam's 'Maps of the Fenland', *The Victoria History of the Counties of England: Huntingdonshire* Vol. 3 (1936)).

Canal Plans

Skills acquired in the execution of river navigation plans paved the way for the canal maps of the second half of the eighteenth century. Indeed, many engineers (not least Brindley) were commissioned to both types of project, so that the plans exhibit a continuity of both scope and design. Canal maps continued to be engraved by the leading craftsmen of the day for distribution to promoters and shareholders, or were reproduced in periodicals such as the *Gentleman's Magazine*. John Cary even published an 'atlas' of these plans entitled *Inland Navigation; or Select Plans of the Several Navigable Canals, throughout Great Britain* . . . (1795) on a standard scale of about half an inch to one mile. As several alternative routes were usually canvassed, the unsuccessful canals also produced their crop of plans now of value to the local historian. This is illustrated in Lancashire, for example, by V. I. Tomlinson's 'Salford Activities connected with the Bridgewater canal', *Transactions of the Lancashire and Cheshire Antiquarian Society* Vol. 66 (1956) and by J. R. Harris's 'Liverpool Canal Controversies 1769-1772', *The Journal of Transport History* Vol. 2 (1955-56). Such projects are also a source of historical misinterpretation, since many maps show the *intended*, not the completed route, and all should be checked against other evidence.

The large-scale deposited plans, discussed by Hadfield in 'Sources for the History of British Canals', *The Journal of Transport History* Vol. 2 (1955-56), were surveyed not only when a canal was first constructed, but when a branch was added, or even modest alterations made to its route; moreover, at the time of takeover by a competing railway company, canals were also surveyed along with the railway where the two routes lay side by side. All these plans covered a strip of land at least a field or so wide on either side of the waterway, furnishing evidence of roads and footpaths, buildings, field names, industrial sites and, in conjunction with a book of reference or a table on the map, lists of owners and occupiers and sometimes land use (Plate 6). Additional features included town plans or perhaps the grounds of an important landowner inset at a larger scale, sections showing the elevation of the proposed route, and incidental information such as the estimated costs of the scheme, tidal levels where relevant, sometimes a triangular table of distances applied to the canal system, and plans and occasional drawings for tunnels and bridges. For some localities these may be the most detailed contemporary maps available.

Many canals were specifically promoted to serve the industrial regions of Britain, and canal plans are therefore an important source for industrial sites. To give but one instance, a 'Plan of the Proposed Navigable Canal, between the River Kennet at Newbury . . . and the River Avon at Bath', surveyed by John Rennie in 1793, and engraved by William Faden, provided in passing a map of the distribution of working coalpits in the Somerset coalfield.

There are also several series of maps of the canal network of Britain (or its regions) as a whole. A number of these maps accompanied the standard contemporary histories such as J. Phillip's *A General History of Inland Navigation, Foreign, and Domestic* (first edition, 1792) or J. Priestley's *Historical Account of the Navigable Rivers, Canals, and Railways throughout Great Britain* (first edition, 1831; new edition, 1967). They must be used with caution, however, because of the practice of incorporating projected canals alongside those which were actually constructed; this indeed is a generic problem in such canal and railway maps, and also in the county maps of the period (see p. 70). The stock-in-trade of several London map-sellers and engravers, including Cary, William Faden and John Andrews, also included general maps of the inland navigations, and even the canal engineers dabbled in general map-making. James Brindley, for instance, prepared *A Plan of the Navigable Canals now making in the Inland Parts of the Kingdom* . . . (1769), which was later revised by Robert Whitworth—another prominent canal engineer. In the nineteenth century one of the more reliable series of maps to include canals was prepared by George Bradshaw; it was issued for different regions of Great Britain (as *G.B.s Map of Canals, Navigable Rivers, Railways etc. in the Southern Counties of England*, c. 1830), but the series was to attain even greater popularity as the railway age matured.

The cartographic evidence for the study of railways, continuing that already described for canals, is summarised by Jack Simmonds in *The Railways of Britain* (1961); a more detailed account of deposited railway plans appeared in his 'Railway History in Local Records', *The Journal of Transport History* Vol. 1 (1954-55). These contributions were however written for the railway historian and the value of railway maps in other branches of local history should not be overlooked.

The deposited plans, made when a railway company wanted to construct, alter, or extend a public railway, are a good general cartographic source— especially before the publication of the local large-scale Ordnance Survey plan and, afterwards, for providing data *between* editions of the official maps. The fact that many schemes never left the drawing board does not diminish the value of the associated plans. Limits vary, but engineers often extended their survey for a quarter of a mile or so from the line. We are thus endowed with a detailed sample of nineteenth-century landscape: in addition to the usual features some plans record the still-unenclosed strips of the open fields; others, as on the principal coalfields, a whole range of industrial sites. Where a railway penetrated a built-up area, or a terminus was to be constructed, the plan was on a larger scale. Plans were accompanied by books of reference, containing data on individual fields, and also by longitudinal sections (compulsory after 1838) which were the result of precise levelling and terrain study. Sometimes, too, the records may include other graphic materials such as designs for bridges, viaducts and stations, whose scope is illustrated by the Brunel manuscripts now preserved in the Library of the University of Bristol. On the question of reliability we may note that deposited railway plans had to form the basis of legislation, and were liable to the exhaustive scrutiny of any opposition, so that they may be rated as a relatively accurate cadastral record. Sometimes a company had to deposit several sets of plans, each modified, before one was finally accepted.

General maps to indicate a provisional railway route, and designed to promote shareholders, are in a different category. Their value is as background to the project, rather than as an original source of topographical evidence. The British Museum has a large collection of these 'prospectus' maps (in 8 volumes at Maps 18. c. 1) and it is clear that the majority were copied from pre-existing small-scale maps, and although lithographed or engraved, were often executed in a sketchy manner, so that some lacked even a scale. It is not unusual to find extra facts on the face of a map, such as the population and industries of the towns to be served, or the comparative mileages by rival routes.

Amongst the series of maps recording the overall growth of the railway system at a national and regional level three categories are useful to the local historian. First, railways continued to be added to some series of county maps; the firm of G. F. Cruchley, tor instance, by taking lithographic transfers from copper-plates acquired from Cary, was able to maintain a series of county maps showing the railways constructed, projected or under construction to the 1870s. Secondly, up to c. 1890, railway detail was added periodically to the successive electrotype printings of the Old Series Ordnance Survey one-inch maps of England and Wales (now reprinted with bibliographical notes by J. B. Harley, by David and Charles Ltd.). Thirdly, the railway maps published by John Airey from 1869 onwards, and later taken over by the former Railway Clearing House, are also reliable; they are described by D. Garnett in 'The Railway Maps of Zachary Macaulay and John Airey', Railway and Canal Historical Society Journal Vol. 5 (1959). They cover Britain, either as a whole or in separate regions, and although the topographical base of the maps is taken from the Ordnance Survey, the specialised railway information is of a primary nature. The lines of each railway company are distinguished by a different colour; all stations and the distances between them are marked; the complexity of railway junctions was shown by separate diagrams on a larger scale; inland navigations were also depicted and each series was regularly revised. On the matter of company ownership the maps acquired official standing (reflected in their title, as the 'Official Railway Map of the East of England'), and may be regarded as authoritative.

The commercial map publishers also issued railway maps—ranging from small maps for inclusion in timetables and railway guides to more ambitious wall maps—in great numbers. Bradshaw's maps have already been noted, but other compilations such as the Map of England and Wales showing the Railways, Canals, and Inland Navigations, published in 1852 for the use of the Committee of the Privy Council for Trade, and Macaulay's Station Map of England and Wales (editions from 1851 onwards) are also useful in showing the network in one document.

The maps and plans discussed above, depicting the major transport media, do not exhaust historical maps of communications. The plans of urban and suburban tramway systems (at first steam or horse-drawn and later electric) have already been noted, and other types can only be mentioned briefly. Taking historical precedence over railways were the horse-drawn tramways and mineral lines important in the early development of the coalfields. Some were too insignificant to appear on medium-scale maps, and, as in south Northumberland, they were often privately run by the colliery owners, and plans were not necessarily deposited by Act of Parliament. Some large-scale engineering plans of tramways have, however, found their way into local record offices; and others are depicted in conjunction with canal schemes— that is, where the tramway was designed to serve as a canal feeder (various examples are noted in The Canals of South Wales and the Border (1960) by Charles Hadfield). There are no series of small-scale maps of these tramway networks such as survive for canals and railways, although they were occasionally the subject of regional maps such as the 'Plan of the Collieries on the River Tyne and Wear . . . by John Gibson, 1788', which shows waggon ways and their length between pit and staith. Industrial tramways were also surveyed for the better county maps of the early nineteenth century.

5 Marine charts

The primary purpose of a marine chart is to show hydrographical detail including the high-water line, low-water features such as sand banks, mud banks and rocks, soundings and fathom lines, recognised anchorages and the position of known wrecks and other hazards, and navigational aids such as buoys, beacons and lighthouses. Land detail is shown only insofar as it assists navigation—to fix position from seaward by reference to prominent hills and buildings, or to identify the coast by its silhouette and physiographic character—as in cliffs, sand dunes or marsh. In view of its specialised nature the marine chart might not seem to furnish significant evidence for the local historian.

This conclusion would be unjustified. The deeply-indented coastline of the British Isles is nearly 5,000 miles in length, and impinges on hundreds of local communities for which marine charts record detailed evidence from the sixteenth century to the present day. Most early charts depict inshore waters, and we may note that many marine surveyors, especially in the eighteenth and early nineteenth century, were almost as concerned with mapping land features as the bed of the sea (George Thomas, for example, in his survey of the Shetlands, completed for the Admiralty in 1834, went so far as to record the archaeology and geology of the country). This emphasis is the local historian's gain. But apart from purely local information, marine charts illuminate several important national themes—such as the periodic fortification of the Channel coast against invasion or the economic history of the sea-borne trade through the age of sail to that of steam.

BIBLIOGRAPHIES OF MARINE CHARTS

A good starting point for the local historian is A. H. W. Robinson's *Marine Cartography in Britain* (1962), providing a concise history from Tudor to Victorian times, and a number of basic lists of early charts of British home waters. These invaluable lists enumerate manuscript charts of the Tudor cartographers, charts of Greenvile Collins and John Adair, seventeenth-century charts, surveys and charts of Murdoch Mackenzie (senior), charts and surveys of the 'amateur' hydrographers, other published charts and manuscript surveys of the eighteenth century, manuscript harbour plans and charts of the military engineers, charts and surveys undertaken by the early Admiralty surveyors, publications of the private chart-sellers, official surveys of the Admiralty Hydrographic Office, and other official surveys during the period 1800-50. For each chart the location in a major repository is given, and the book is illustrated by a representative selection of reproductions (supplemented by the examples in Mary Blewitt's Surveys of the Seas (1957).

No other union list of such charts is in print—although a short list of Scottish charts appeared in The Early Maps of Scotland (2nd ed., 1936)—and the next stage may be to investigate the resources of the main collections. Amongst these, the British Museum is pre-eminent, and its highlights were reviewed by R. A. Skelton in 'The Hydrographic Collections of the British Museum', Journal of the Institute of Navigation Vol. IX (1956), and in 'King George III's Maritime Collection', British Museum Quarterly Vol. XVIII (1953). The scope of the collection is international, but in the Catalogue of Printed Maps . . . (1967), entries for printed charts of home waters are consolidated under England, Coasts, and so on; other local charts are administered in the Department of Manuscripts and are listed in the Catalogue of Manuscript Maps, Charts and Plans . . . (reprinted, 1962), and in continuing Catalogues of Additions to Manuscripts.

Other important collections are those of the Hydrographic Department of the Admiralty[1], lacking a published catalogue, although some charts of British coasts are listed in A Summary of Selected Manuscript Documents of Historic Importance Preserved in the Archives of the Department (Hydrographic Department, Professional Paper No. 13, 1950); the National Maritime Museum at Greenwich, where a printed catalogue is in preparation, and meanwhile a 'Summary List of Manuscript Sea Charts and Pilot Books Down to 1700 . . . ' is available in typescript; the Bodleian Library; the Public Record Office, where many marine plans related to harbour fortifications are listed in Maps and Plans in the Public Record Office 1 . . . (1967); and the Royal Geographical Society, the maritime holdings of which were described by G. R. Crone in 'Early Books and Charts in the Royal Geographical Society's Collection', Journal of the Institute of Navigation Vol. 6 (1953). These larger collections are supplemented at a regional and local level, by the holdings of the National Library of Wales and the National Library of Scotland, by materials in the archives and libraries of port towns and by charts in private collections such as that of Lord Salisbury at Hatfield House.

The study of the printed marine atlases and charts relating to the British Isles is hampered by a dearth of carto-bibliographical studies. The majority

[1] Hydrographic Department, Ministry of Defence, Taunton, Somerset.

ran to multiple editions, with each copper-plate liable to substitution and revision, yet few of these variants have been identified, and their history as printed documents is relatively unknown. A number of editions of the major atlases are noted in A. H. W. Robinson (op. cit.), and in R. V. Tooley's *Maps and Map-Makers* (3rd ed., 1970); otherwise we may obtain guidance from the British Museum *Catalogue* which distinguishes between editions in its possession; and charts of Dutch origin are listed in C. Koeman's definitive descriptive bibliography *Atlantes Neerlandici* (Vol. I, 1967).

With the appearance of the official charts of the Hydrographic Department of the Admiralty (founded in 1795), the complexity of the main era of private chart publishing is much reduced. Unlike the early printings of Ordnance Survey maps, of which there is no official record of publication, early Admiralty charts are more easily dated. L. S. Dawson's *Memoirs of Hydrography* (2 vols., 1885), continued as *The Admiralty Hydrographic Service 1795-1919* (1967) by Vice-Admiral Sir Archibald Day, provide a well-documented narrative of the progress of marine survey, with year by year summaries of the 'principal surveys'. But of greater bibliographical value, the official *Catalogues of Charts, Plans, views and Sailing Directions . . . published by the Admiralty* (the titles vary somewhat) commence in 1825 (the British Museum copies begin in 1829), and although they do not appear annually until 1886, gaps of two or more years are rare.[1] After 1839 they list charts by a standard number, giving size, scale, surveyor, and in successive issues, notes of corrections and revisions accomplished since the last printing. With Admiralty Charts there is the further simplification that the sheet lines have remained relatively unchanged since their inception, except where certain charts have lapsed, and their numbers have been re-allocated. Changes have, however, occurred in the arrangement of the *Catalogues*, so that charts of the British Isles now appear in a different 'Section' than was formerly the case.

THE DEVELOPMENT OF MARINE CHARTS

The main stages in the development of marine charts mirror the evolution of British local and regional maps as a whole. In the middle ages there were no indigenous British schools of chart-making, and the only marine depiction of the coasts of Britain, described by M. C. Andrews in 'The British Isles in the nautical charts of the XIVth and XVth centuries', *The Geographical Journal* Vol. 68 (1926), appeared in portolan or compass charts compiled by European hydrographers. The study of this material has long been eased by the facsimiles gathered by A. E. Nordenskiöld in *Periplus; an essay on the early history of charts and sailing directions* (Stockholm, 1897), and while some of his conclusions are no longer acceptable, the collection remains indispensable. Relatively few portolan charts have survived (about twenty for the fourteenth

[1] Only in 1833-38, 1842-45, 1850-51, 1853-54, 1858-59 and 1873-74.

53

century) and they are small in scale, often with heavily conventionalised coastlines, and little detail other than the courses of a few rivers, and names and symbols for ports. Yet they should not be dismissed as entirely devoid of local data. Even unpromising material may disguise a critical fact, as G. de Boer recently demonstrated in a discussion of 'The Historical Variations of Spurn Point: the Evidence of Early Maps' in The Geographical Journal Vol. 135 (1969); one of the helpful clues, albeit far from unambiguous, in locating Ravenserodd (Yorkshire, E.R.), a medieval port which appeared in 1235 and disappeared about 1360, was its inclusion on portolan charts of the later middle ages.

Alongside portolans, and indeed all subsequent charts, the historian should consider the collateral evidence of written (later printed) sailing directions— often known as 'rutters'. An early-fifteenth-century example, Sailing Directions for the Circumnavigation of England, has been published by the Hakluyt Society (Vol. 79, 1889), but from the seventeenth century onwards, sailing directions were commonly issued with each chart, and as integral parts of marine atlases. The first English and French sailing directions have been edited (in facsimile) by D. W. Waters, The Rutters of the Sea (Yale University Press, 1967). They often supplement chart evidence and their descriptions of navigable channels and landmarks on shore may be unique. The water-colour sketches and views of land and harbours—some made by special marine artists, others by serving naval officers—can also be a useful adjunct to the data in orthodox charts.

Tudor and Stuart Hydrography

An important source book for understanding the charts of this period is The Art of Navigation in England in Elizabethan and Early Stuart Times (1958), by David W. Waters, which includes 'An Index of Navigational MSS and works printed before 1640'. The earliest attempts by Englishmen to chart their own coasts in fact date to the reign of Henry VIII, when a group of military engineers, such as Richard Lee, John Rodgers and Richard Popinjay, whose careers—with many others—are summarised by E. G. R. Taylor, The Mathematical Practitioners of Tudor and Stuart England (1954), were commissioned to maintain coastal defences and to effect harbour improvements. One by-product of their work was a series of bird's-eye view plans, especially of the harbours and coastlands of the English channel, probably drawn from ships anchored offshore. Such a military plan of the coast and hinterland of South Devon between Exmouth and the headland of Tor, is illustrated by Edward Lynam in The Map-Maker's Art (1953), and A. H. W. Robinson (op. cit.) reproduces comparable examples of Harwich, Jersey, Poole Harbour and Dover; plans of the last-named—especially numerous—are discussed by A. Macdonald in 'Plans of Dover Harbour in the Sixteenth Century', Archaeologia Cantiana Vol. 49 (1937).

By the last quarter of the sixteenth century local charts were becoming more sophisticated and instead of exaggerated perspective drawings of land features, truly hydrographic information, including details of sand banks, submarine rocks, soundings and anchorages, as well as landing places, quays, harbour works and beacons, begin to appear. Even so, and although new chart-makers such as Robert Adams, Robert Norman and William Borough came to the fore, their work remained in manuscript and was confined to the busier estuaries of South-East England.

The first printed sea atlas, and first to show the British coasts, was the *Spieghel der Zeevaerdt* (Leiden, 1584-85) by Lucas Janszoon Waghenaer, an English edition of which appeared only two years later as *The Mariners Mirror* (1588). This milestone in chart-making has a large literature, recently summarised by C. Koeman in 'Lucas Janszoon Waghenaer: Sixteenth Century Marine Cartographer', *The Geographical Journal* Vol. 131 (1965), and in 1964 the *Spieghel* became twice available in facsimile with introductions by C. Koeman and R. A. Skelton respectively, while *The Mariners Mirror* is also available in a facsimile (*Theatrum Orbis Terrarum*, 1966).

Waghenaer's charts were designed especially for pilotage, and although on relatively small scales, estuaries and harbour approaches were enlarged in comparison with the rest of the coast. Profiles or elevations of coastal scenery, providing prominent landmarks for mariners to take their bearings from, thereafter standard to most charts, and written sailing directions accompany the work; the latter include notes on the products of the hinterland and the commerce of the ports. Sailing ships, decorating open waters on some charts, record regional types of vessels—as the herring fleets off the coast of East Anglia.

The Dutch map publishers, as in the field of regional cartography, dominated the marine atlas market during the first half of the seventeenth century. The material assembled by Waghenaer remained basic to most collections of charts (just as the name 'Waggoner' survived to describe them); but in some workshops, notably in that of Willem Janszoon Blaeu, charts were systematically revised from the journals, logs and observations of practising mariners. In *The Light of Navigation* (1612), for example, reproduced by Theatrum Orbis Terrarum in 1964 with an introduction by R. A. Skelton, new data on buoys, beacons and lights, and enlarged sailing directions, appear on some English charts. For the local historian, however, the record remains thin in detail and patchy in geographical coverage.

Restoration Hydrography

The seventeenth century maintained the Tudor initiative in local chart-making mainly through the enterprise of resident pilots and masters, and officers in Trinity House and the Custom Service. Yet the activity was regionally unbalanced (there are no local charts of north-west England for the period), unco-ordinated, and charts circulated only in manuscript—from the quills of such marine draftsmen as Nicholas Comberford. Not until after the

Restoration was there an intensification of other than purely local chart-making; but then a new era begins which has been described by G. P. B. Naish in 'Hydrographic Surveys by Officers of the Navy under the later Stuarts', *Journal of the Institute of Navigation* Vol. 9 (1956).

The first attempt to publish a sea-atlas in England—the *English Pilot* (Book 1, 1671), compiled by John Seller, Hydrographer to Charles II—did little to improve on its Dutch predecessors. Few of the charts and sailing directions—only those of the Thames, Humber and Tyne—were based on original English sources. The majority were printed from a surreptitious purchase of obsolete Dutch copper-plates!

Accordingly the surveys of Captain Greenvile Collins remain unchallenged as the first systematic survey of British coastal waters. He secured the support of the Admiralty and Trinity House, and, beginning in 1681, spent seven years surveying various sections of the coast of England and Wales, the east coast of Scotland, and the Orkney and Shetland Isles. But of the 120 charts he drafted only 48 were published, first singly, and then as *Great Britain's Coasting Pilot* (1693) (Figure 3a). The charts are useful local documents: estuaries and harbours were shown on larger scales, and furnish a wealth of new detail, not only hydrographic, but numerous landmarks on shore. In an age when county mapping was frequently moribund, Collin's charts may provide the best *land* map available in some localities (Plate 7). The *Pilot* ran to over twelve editions up to 1792—a few with new charts added—and a facsimile has been published of the 1753 edition by Mount and Page (Sudbrook Press, Bucks., and G. G. Harrap, London, 1964).

Nor was Collins a lone figure in charting the coasts of Britain in the late-seventeenth century. Edmund Dummer, 'Surveyor of the Navy at Portsmouth', organised 'A Survey of the Ports on the South West coast of England from Dover to Lands-end' (c. 1698). The seventeen plans are the best contemporary representations of some of these harbours. And in Scotland, John Adair was engaged on a marine survey comparable to that of Collins, although his labours were not published until the following century (see A. H. W. Robinson, 'The Charting of the Scottish Coasts', *Scottish Geographical Magazine* Vol. 74 (1958) and 'Two Unrecorded Manuscript Charts by John Adair' *Ibid*. Vol. 75 (1959).

The Eighteenth Century

On several fronts the eighteenth century was one of notable achievement in British chart-making, culminating in the establishment of the Hydrographic Department of the Admiralty (1795). Even if there was no systematic national policy, and charts continued to vary in accuracy, style and amount of detail shown, much of the coast came to be re-charted (or charted for the first time) by surveyors with different objectives and backgrounds. Some work, as earlier, was local in character, and the plans of the military engineers on coastal duty may be especially detailed. The more prolific surveyor-engineers, such as

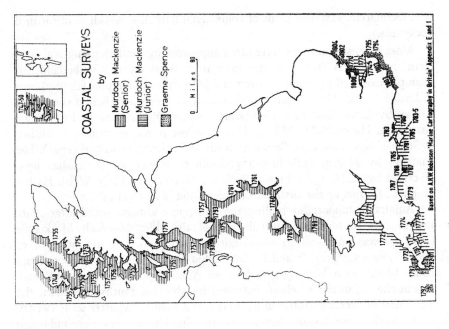

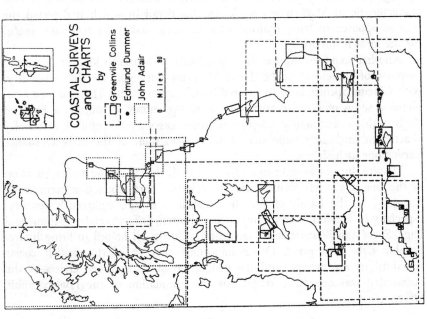

FIGURE 3 (*a* & *b*). Important marine surveys of the late-seventeenth and eighteenth century.

57

J. P. Desmaretz, executed plans of commercial harbours as well as of fortified dockyards.

More extensive surveys were often supported by local shipping and merchant interests. A survey of the coast from Anglesey to Cumberland, for example, executed by Samuel Fearon and John Eyes of Liverpool (1736-7), was dedicated to the 'Mayor and . . . Merchants of Liverpool'. And a competing survey by Lewis Morris, a Holyhead Customs Officer, was limited to the coast from Llandudno to Milford Haven, before it was eventually published as *Plans of Harbours, Bars, Bays and Roads in St. Georges Channel* (1748). The charting by Morris, including a preliminary survey on shore, has been described by A. H. W. Robinson in 'Lewis Morris—An Early Welsh Hydrographer', *Journal of the Institute of Navigation* Vol. 11 (1958).

Admiralty support for hydrographic mapping also improved after 1750, and in this context, the contribution of the elder Murdoch Mackenzie (1712-97) was outstanding. Mackenzie came to notice as the surveyor of *Orcades, or a Geographic and Hydrographic Description of the Orkney and Lewis Islands in 8 Maps* (1750) done on Admiralty commission; and then, also at the Admiralty's behest, extended his charting southwards down the west coast of Scotland (hitherto neglected) and eventually, after some twenty years, reached the Bristol Channel (Figure 3b). The surveys were published in 1776 as *A Maritim Survey of Ireland and West Coast of Britain*, and are distinguished both by their relative detail—many were drafted at a scale of one inch to one mile—and by their accuracy, being the first major British hydrographic survey to be based on a rigid triangulation on shore. One characteristic of Mackenzie's work was the detail in which it depicted the land as opposed to truly hydrographic features, making it especially useful for the local historian.

Another step forward was the appointment of Murdoch Mackenzie, junior (nephew of the elder), to be 'Head Maritime Surveyor' for the Admiralty, with Graeme Spence, later to succeed him, as an assistant. The two men completed a series of detailed surveys around the shores of south-east England (Figure 3b), subsequently adopted in some cases as the official Admiralty charts, and including more coastal detail than some of the early Ordnance Survey one-inch sheets.

Despite the official stake in such enterprises, the engraving and publication of the charts was left to individual surveyors. Chart production accordingly remained in the hands of private map-sellers in the eighteenth century, especially in London, where firms such as Bowen, Jefferys, Faden, Mount and Page, Sayer and Bennett, and Laurie and Whittle, all helped to bring hydrographic data into print. Other important surveys of the British coasts remained in manuscript, and the congestion of unexamined charts at the Admiralty was one basic reason for the foundation of the Hydrographic Office.

Admiralty Charts

After various unsuccessful proposals the Hydrographic Office was established in 1795; a very readable history will be found in Rear-Admiral G. S. Ritchie's *The Admiralty Chart—British Naval Hydrography in the Nineteenth Century* (1967). Alexander Dalrymple, already Hydrographer to the East India Company, was its first head, but not until after the appointment of Thomas Hurd as his successor in 1808 was the department organised to become an efficient chart-making concern from survey to publication. Under Francis Beaufort, whose career has been outlined by K. St. B. Collins, 'Admiral Sir Francis Beaufort', *Journal of the Institute of Navigation* Vol. 11 (1958), the 'Grand Survey of the British Isles' was completed. When Beaufort took over in 1829 there were only 44 Admiralty Charts of the United Kingdom, covering the area from the Wash to Land's End: in 1855, when he retired, no less than 255 charts of home waters were available—virtually a completed coverage of the coast, and appropriate to the rapid growth of steam navigation (Figure 4).

The size and scale of Admiralty charts varied considerably with their scope and purpose, and as the visual indexes to the sheet lines (first published in 1873) make clear the overlap was necessarily much greater than with land maps. Full details appear in the official *Catalogues*, but we may note that harbour plans were on the largest scales (from 10 to 20 inches to one mile and upwards); estuaries, bays and harbour approaches used intermediate scales (from 1 to 10 inches to one mile); and general charts of open coasts were smallest (often below 1 inch to one mile). The earliest printings of the large-scale charts often pre-date the Ordnance Survey large-scale plans for the same area. Moreover, once published, Admiralty charts underwent almost continuous revision where appropriate, published separately from 1857 onwards in the Admiralty Notices to Mariners, as well as appearing on successive 'editions' and 'corrections' of the charts. Changes along the coastline of Britain in the Victorian era and afterwards are thus particularly well documented.

MARINE CHARTS AND THE LOCAL HISTORIAN

We must be aware both of the limitations and the potential of early marine charts. For every locality there will be endemic weaknesses in the chain of evidence they provide: many charts are likely to be unreliable, and some are merely duplicates, the data of which can be discarded. As we have seen, variations in their availability are regional as well as chronological and, especially before 1700, the south-eastern coasts of Britain are far better charted than the north-western.

A basic problem is that of assigning a date to the *content* of a marine chart, in contradistinction to the date of its production. With manuscript charts a lack of contemporaneity is first encountered in the age of the portolan: not only was there a time lag between the acquisition of new facts and their incorporation in the 'standard' chart, but once standardised, a chart

59

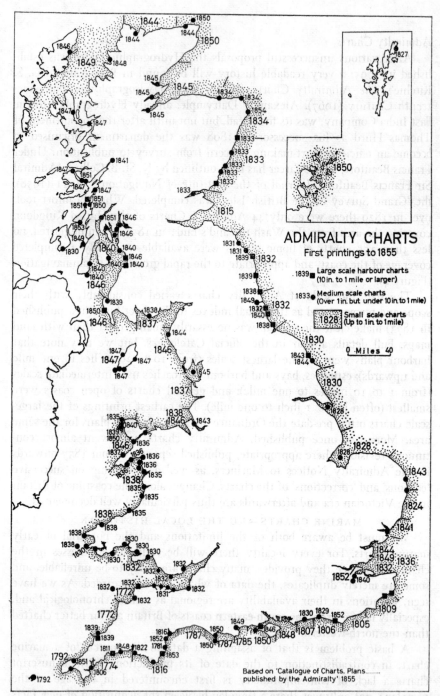

ADMIRALTY CHARTS
First printings to 1855

. 1839 • Large scale harbour charts
(10 in. to 1 mile or larger)

1833 • Medium scale charts
(Over 1 in. but under 10 in. to 1 mile)

1828 Small scale charts
(Up to 1 in. to 1 mile)

0 Miles 40

Based on 'Catalogue of Charts, Plans........
published by the Admiralty' 1855

FIGURE 4. The coverage and chronology of the early Admiralty charts. Dates are of survey; question marks are where the data is ambiguous. Note the importance of the period after 1830 when the 'Grand Survey' of the British Isles was executed.

could remain virtually unaltered even for centuries. The information in each chart must therefore be traced back to its original sources.

With the application of copper-plate printing to the production of marine charts, the difficulties, if anything, were exacerbated. Although many identical copies could now be produced, improving the speed and reliability with which hydrographic information was disseminated, the technique fostered conservatism. A set of copper-plates, properly cared for, had a potentially long life during which a basic design was perpetuated, subject only to local touching-up and revision. This was as true of the Dutch charts of the seventeenth century as of the publications of the London map-sellers in the eighteenth: commercial considerations came first and all drew freely, usually without acknowledgement, on the limited range of common authorities. Lack of new information was no deterrent to republication. Greenvile Collins' *Great Britain's Coasting Pilot*, for instance, received only five new charts in the course of a century.

Then there is the question of absolute accuracy. Many of the pre-Admiralty charts were plainly unreliable. If we compare a series of charts of the same area through time, no doubt their accuracy will be seen to improve, as A. H. W. Robinson has demonstrated by comparing outlines of the Orkneys in charts of 1646, 1693 and 1750 with a modern chart. However, as A. P. Carr reminds us in 'Cartographic Record and Historical Accuracy', *Geography* Vol. 47 (1962), even the latest Admiralty chart may not be unimpeachable in the light of detailed local research. Differences between early charts of similar date must also be carefully collated, and answers sought to the questions how and why they are different. Contemporary users had few illusions about the shortcomings of deficient charts, and their comments—such as those of Samuel Pepys who as Secretary to the Navy criticised the work of Greenvile Collins—may help to put us on our guard.

The users of early charts must also be conversant with the basic techniques of their construction. As with land maps, surveying methods often put limits to the accuracy attainable, and various sources, such as accounts of surveying practice found in the prefatory remarks to marine atlases, or in textbooks, such as the elder Murdoch Mackenzie's *A Treatise on Maritim Surveying . . .* (1774) will assist in evaluation. There are also special problems, and, as R. A. Skelton has demonstrated in a wider context, in *Looking at an Early Map* (University of Kansas Libraries, 1965), historians ignorant of these matters have fallen victims to misinterpretation. Before we use early charts, for example, we must be aware that their meridians and outlines are likely to be uncorrected for magnetic variation, and will therefore have to be rotated (according to the known magnetic declination of the place and date) in order to make a valid comparison with a modern outline. Similarly the question of projection, a matter of great concern to hydrographers, must be considered when examining charts. Unlike many local and regional maps on land where projection was usually ignored, charts (especially after 1700) were constructed on either Mercator's projection or, with large-scale harbour plans, on a modified gnomonic projection. Suitable allowances must be made if comparisons are sought with maps or charts on different projections.

On the other hand, we should avoid being pedantic about chart evidence. Accuracy is often important only in the light of its historical relevance and not for its own sake. Everything should not be measured by modern standards: to answer some questions a crude map may well suffice. The local studies to which marine charts have been harnessed include a wide range of problems which rely on establishing successive changes to a shoreline, to sandbanks and navigable channels, to the edge of saltmarsh or of sand dune. Some of these studies (the province of the coastal geomorphologist) may be concerned with physiographic change as an end in itself. Many more will be exploring the inter-relationship between physical change and the social and economic history of a local community. Yet others will be topographical in bias—to help locate a decayed haven, a parish eroded by the sea, a chapel engulfed by sand, or to fix the site of a lighthouse once crucial to navigation. Not least, local scholarship is awakening to an archaeological potential in the numerous wrecks located on our early charts; and for this purpose, too, a good grounding in some of the principles underlying the reliability of chart evidence is essential.

6 County maps

From Elizabethan to mid-Victorian times the county was the basic unit of regional mapping in Britain, and the county atlas the commonest format of publication. Most counties have well over a hundred separate maps—in the sense of individually engraved copper-plates—and with numerous variant states being known of each plate. In addition, there are district maps, such as the maps of the 'Country around' London and other cities, and printed maps of areas such as the Fens. As a result many historians will be more familiar with the county map than with some of the other maps described in this *Guide*. A blend of decorative attractiveness and historical interest has led to their inclusion in many local history studies, and, recently, as if coming of age, they have illustrated the *Victoria County History of England* (Essex, Vol. 5, 1966; Staffordshire, Vol. 8, 1963).

Even so, the tendency has been to value them more as evocative illustrations than as primary sources of evidence. This is unfortunate. County maps contain an important corpus of information about the changing landscape of Britain since Tudor times. Because the coverage is national, and usually available for a succession of dates, they provide control and a framework for more fragmentary topographical sources, especially when they become more detailed in the eighteenth century. We must indeed be on our guard against the many plagiarised maps amongst the handful of original surveys for each county, but even such a disadvantage is outweighed by their overall usefulness. For recording a fairly complete distribution of several features in the countryside there may be no alternative source. To give a simple example, what other single document could give such a full inventory of early windmills as some of our Georgian county surveys? (See, for instance, the map of Lincolnshire windmills, *Transactions of the Newcomen Society*, Vol. 29 (1953-54).) Or how else, as J. T. Coppock re-emphasises in 'Maps as Sources for the Study of Land Use in the Past', *Imago Mundi*, Vol. 22 (1969), can we reconstruct the broad distribution of cultivated and uncultivated land in the eighteenth century but from county maps? The student of boundaries, communications, industrial sites, parks, village morphology, placenames, and family history may locate important data on the maps of his county.

BIBLIOGRAPHIES OF COUNTY MAPS

The enthusiasm of collectors (more than of historians) has resulted in substantial progress in the bibliographical analysis of county maps. A start was made by Richard Gough, whose *British Topography* (2 vols., 1780) listed many of the county maps published by his day. Gough's labours were not however systematically built upon, and only with the publication of Sir H. G. Fordham's 'Hertfordshire Maps; a Descriptive Catalogue, 1579-1900', *Transactions Hertfordshire Nat. Hist. Soc.* (1901-3-5 and 1907), was a blueprint for modern cartobibliography set down.

Three types of bibliography are available. First, there are comprehensive national bibliographies, the most fundamental of which, inspired by Fordham, and still a basic reference tool, is Thomas Chubb's *The Printed Maps in the Atlases of Great Britain and Ireland: a bibliography 1579-1870* (1927, reprinted 1966). Since Chubb's day, however, a great deal of work has been done and new maps and atlases have come to light. The most recent researches have been incorporated in a completely new work, *County Atlases of the British Isles 1579-1850. A bibliography*, compiled by R. A. Skelton (Map Collectors Series, Parts I-IV, 1964-68); the material covering 1579-1703 is now published separately (Carta Press, 1970). A short list of *Maps of Wales and Welsh Cartographers*, by Olwen Caradoc Evans, was also published by the Map Collectors' Circle (1964); and a basic list of maps of Scottish counties appears in *The Early Maps of Scotland* (2nd ed., 1936). For larger-scale county maps, many at scales of one inch to one mile and over, Elizabeth M. Rodger's *The Large Scale County Maps of the British Isles 1596-1850 A Union List* (Bodleian Library, 1960) is invaluable; and is supplemented by detailed descriptions of individual maps in E. J. Huddy's (unfortunately unpublished) 'Early Printed Topographical Maps of the Counties of England and Wales' (University of London Thesis, 1960).

Secondly, there are bibliographies of the printed maps of individual counties. In England these date from the pioneer list of H. G. Fordham (finally republished as *Hertfordshire maps: a descriptive catalogue of the maps of the county 1579-1900* (1914)), to the most recent, *A Descriptive List of the Printed Maps of Shropshire A.D. 1577-1900* (1959), by Geoffrey C. Cowling. But there are still many counties without bibliographies (Figure 5), and the quality of existing work is uneven. Some county lists, such as F. A. Wadsworth's 'Nottinghamshire maps of the 16th, 17th and 18th centuries: their makers and engravers', *Transactions of the Thoroton Society* Vol. 34 (1930) and *Leicestershire maps: a brief Survey* (1947), by Basil L. Gimson and Percy Russell, describe only highlights; and the most systematic disciples of Fordham were Thomas Chubb and Harold Whitaker. The first-named com-

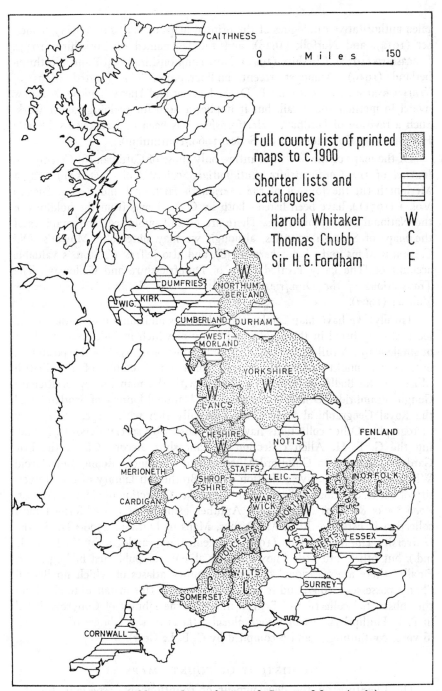

FIGURE 5. Bibliographies of Printed County Maps (1969)

piled authoritative catalogues of the printed maps of Wiltshire (1911), Somerset (1914), and Norfolk (1928); and the last-named of Yorkshire (1933), Lancashire (1938), Cheshire (1942), Northamptonshire (1948) and Northumberland (1949). Amongst recent bibliographies, *The Printed Maps of Warwickshire* . . . (1959), by P. D. A. Harvey and Harry Thorpe, is a new model in method and detail, but it implies a need for re-doing earlier work. Such a revision of Fordham's *Hertfordshire* has been undertaken by Donald Hodson (Map Collectors' Circle Series, 1969, continuing).

Of the maps of the Welsh counties, only those of Cardigan (in *Ceredigion, Journal of the Cardiganshire Antiquarian Society* Vol. 2 (1955)) and of Merioneth (in the *Journal of the Merioneth Historical and Record Society* Vol. 1 (1951)), have been listed—both by G. M. Lewis from the holdings of the National Library of Wales. There are no full published bibliographies of the maps of Scottish counties, although we may note John Mowat's, *Old Caithness Maps and Mapmakers* (1938), and also Jeffrey C. Stone's valuable account of 'The Early Printed Maps of Dumfriesshire and Galloway', *The Transactions of the Dumfriesshire and Galloway Natural History Society* Vol. 44 (1967).

Thirdly, we have map catalogues of libraries and museums, national and local, already listed in the *Guide*, and many of which include county atlases or single maps. A full list would incorporate most recognised local repositories; but, as we might anticipate, certain collections, notably of the British Museum, the Bodleian Library—endowed with the map library of Richard Gough—Cambridge University Library, the National Library of Scotland, and the Royal Geographical Society, are especially rich with respect to county cartography. Other collections have been boosted by special deposits, including the G. E. H. Allen collection in Lancashire Record Office, the Eric Gardner collection in Guildford Museum and Muniment Room, and Harold Whitaker's representative collection in the Brotherton Library of the University of Leeds, described in *The Harold Whitaker Collection of County Atlases, Road-Books & Maps* . . . (1947). Another example of a well-formed local collection is listed by Ruth M. Turner, *Maps of Durham 1576-1872 in the University Library Durham* (1954, supplementary catalogue by A. I. Doyle n.d.), but others are little known in the absence of published bibliography. Finally, there are occasional editions of county atlases of which no British library possesses a copy, and it may be worthwhile (for instance) to check on the substantial collection of British atlases in the Library of Congress, listed in P. L. Phillips' *A List of Geographical Atlases in the Library of Congress* (6 vols., continuing, 5 and 6 compiled by C. E. Le Gear).

THE HISTORY OF COUNTY MAPS

The literature on the development of county maps, especially for the period before 1700, is larger than for most other classes of local maps, doubtless because of their longstanding interest to collectors, although many recent facsimile publications have been aimed at historians. There is no standard history of the county maps of Britain. They are generously treated in R. V. Tooley's *Maps and Map-Makers* (Third ed. 1970) with a useful bibliography, but local historians will find Harry Thorpe's account of 'The personality of Warwickshire reflected in its printed maps' (in Harvey and Thorpe op. cit.) especially helpful in suggesting topographical data on maps of their own county. For Cheshire, J. B. Harley has described the more important county maps likely to be of interest in local studies (*Cheshire Round* Vol. 1, Nos. 6, 7, 8, 9 (1966-68)).

The Elizabethan period

With one or two exceptions, there are no separate maps of the regions of Britain before Elizabethan times, and the most detailed local depictions appear on maps of the country as a whole. The development of such maps is admirably portrayed by the facsimiles (with notes by G. R. Crone) in *Early Maps of the British Isles A.D. 1000 - A.D. 1579* (Royal Geographical Society, 1961). The real beginnings of regional cartography emerge after 1550, and are discussed by Edward Lynam in 'English maps and map-makers of the sixteenth century', *Geographical Journal* Vol. 116 (1950, reprinted in *The Map Maker's Art*, 1953). Laurence Nowell had proposed a series of county maps in 1563 (two sets of maps from his pen survive in manuscript), but the work of Christopher Saxton, based on a survey of England and Wales, and engraved between 1574 and 1579, first gave substance to the county format which was to be so enduring. The two basic accounts of Saxton's work are still Sir H. G. Fordham's *Christopher Saxton of Dunningley: his life and work* (Leeds, 1928) and Edward Lynam's introduction to the British Museum coloured facsimile of *An Atlas of England and Wales. The Maps of Christopher Saxton engraved 1574-1579* (1934, introduction revised 1939). Neither attempts to analyse Saxton's treatment of local topography, and a complementary approach is found in G. Manley's 'Saxton's survey of Northern England', *Geographical Journal* Vol. 83 (1932).

Almost immediately contemporary map-makers began either to copy or to modify Saxton's work. Directly plagiarised (and reduced) versions of Saxton are listed in standard bibliographies; but, amongst the innovators, we may note John Norden whose output is listed in R. A. Skelton's *Decorative Printed Maps of the 15th to 18th Centuries* (1952); the 'Anonymous' cartographer, now identified as William Smith the herald, author of twelve county maps (see R. A. Skelton, 'Four English County Maps, 1602-3', *British Museum Quarterly*, Vol. 12 (1960)); and Philip Symonson, an estate surveyor, whose map of Kent (1596) was remarkably detailed for this date. A good selection of the work of these cartographers, introduced by Edward Heawood, was

67

issued in facsimile as *English County maps in the collection of the Royal Geographical Society* (R.G.S., 1932).

In Scotland, too, Saxton's *Atlas* inspired emulation, and Timothy Pont, a Caithness clergyman, made surveys of much of Scotland between c.1590-1610. His techniques, however, were relatively crude; and in any case the drafts remained in manuscript until edited by Robert and James Gordon of Straloch, for eventual publication by Blaeu in 1654. This complex story has been most recently unravelled (with new evidence) by R. A. Skelton in *County Atlases of the British Isles* (Part III, Map Collectors' Series, 1968); and by D. G. Moir and R. A. Skelton in 'New Light on the first atlas of Scotland', *Scottish Geographical Magazine* Vol. 84 (1968).

The seal to this pioneer phase of county cartography was grandly set by John Speed's *Theatre of the Empire of Great Britain* (1611)—the earliest published atlas of the British Isles. Although the maps were not based on original survey (unlike the inset town plans), but were compiled from Saxton, Norden and Smith (amongst others), they were well designed and were the first to show the boundaries of the hundreds. They have been reprinted (in part) as *John Speed's England: a coloured facsimile of the maps and text from the Theatre of the Empire of Great Britain . . . 1611* (1953), and edited by J. Arlott.

The mid-seventeenth century

In the half-century centred on 1650 county map-makers lived off the fat of the Tudor period. No original surveys were undertaken. Not only were new editions struck from obsolete plates without significant revision—Saxton's *Atlas* for instance was reprinted in 1645—but newly-engraved maps were likewise compiled from the same dated sources. Only in design and decoration was the county map developing as the Dutch geographical publishers acquired a dominating share of English map production. The county maps in the rival atlases of Joan Blaeu and Jan Jansson (both entitled *Theatrum Orbis Terrarum*, and first published in 1645 and 1646 respectively) were particularly splendid examples of decorative cartography. Yet the historian should view them rather as copies of Speed—in the case of Jansson with the place-names imperfectly transcribed. Blaeu's publication of the Scottish surveys of Timothy Pont—currently reprinting in facsimile by John Bartholomew & Son Ltd.—provides an exception in which Dutch maps mark a real advance over the *data* of pre-existing printed maps. A full descriptive bibliography of the Dutch maps of British counties will be incorporated in C. Koeman's *Atlantes Neerlandici* (Vol. 1, 1967).

Restoration maps

In county mapmaking, as in cartography in general, the Restoration saw a quickening interest in scientific survey. The new intellectual climate was symbolised by the Royal Society, and some of its connections with cartography are highlighted by E. G. R. Taylor in 'Robert Hooke and the cartographical projects of the late-seventeenth century', The Geographical Journal Vol. 90 (1937). Several ambitious schemes for the improvement of existing county maps were launched—including John Adams' triangulation of England and Wales, proposals by John Seller and Moses Pitt to produce new English atlases (the latter described by E. G. R. Taylor, ' "The English Atlas" of Moses Pitt, 1680-83', The Geographical Journal Vol. 95 (1940), and John Ogilby's projected sequel to Britannia which was to include a series of county surveys. Few of these promises were fulfilled. The legacy of the Restoration period is only a handful of new county surveys—such as Oxfordshire (1677), and Staffordshire (1682), by the natural historian Robert Plot; Ogilby's Essex (1678), and Middlesex (1677); and Seller's Hertfordshire (1676), Kent (1680), and Middlesex (1680). Yet cartographical thinking had been regenerated. Dissatisfaction with re-issues of Tudor maps was more widely voiced. Robert Morden, in introducing the county maps accompanying Edmund Gibson's 1695 edition of Camden's Britannia, deliberately asserted that they were ' . . . all new engrav'd, either according to Surveys never before publish'd, or according to such as have been made since Saxton and Speed'. His good intentions were presumably bedevilled only by the lack of such surveys for the majority of counties.

The eighteenth century

The eighteenth century witnessed a revolution in county map-making. In technique most of the maps came to be based on scientific triangulation. In scale nearly every county was increased to one inch to one mile or larger. In content an extended alphabet of conventional signs represented the landscape in unprecedented detail. Nearly the whole of Britain was thus re-surveyed before the Ordnance Survey commenced regular publication of its maps in 1805.

Progress was at first slow and sporadic. In many counties up to 1750 the historian may discover only up-dated versions of Saxton and Speed. Many of the maps of Herman Moll, John Senex and Emanuel Bowen fell into this obsolete category. A survey as technically advanced as Henry Beighton's map of Warwickshire (1725) was exceptional; other maps, such as John Strachey's Somerset (1736), described by J. B. Harley in 'John Strachey of Somerset: an antiquarian cartographer of the early eighteenth century', The Cartographic Journal Vol. 3 (1966), were interesting experiments but failures in practice.

The mid-century marked a turning point. A spate of new surveys were started, described by J. B. Harley in 'The re-mapping of England, 1750-1800', Imago Mundi Vol. XIX (1965). The earliest of these maps, such as those by John Rocque and Isaac Taylor, were independently conceived; but, after 1759, the premiums awarded by the Society of Arts for original county surveys, tended to standardise as well as to encourage geographically separate schemes.

The rapidity of publication (Figure 6) means that for broad areas of Britain we have fairly comparable map evidence for this period. A number of county historical societies — including Ayrshire, Devon, Essex, Gloucestershire, Lancashire and Wiltshire—have republished these maps in facsimile.

The nineteenth century

The foundation of the Ordnance Survey did not spell out immediate redundancy for the private county surveyor. Indeed, it was a recognised function of the Trigonometrical Survey of the Board of Ordnance, to supply the location of trigonometrical points to raise the standard of private cartography. The opportunity was quickly taken. A new map of Herefordshire (1817), for instance, by Henry Price, was 'founded on the Basis of the Trigonometrical Survey of the Kingdom . . . '. But the cartographers to exploit Ordnance data most systematically were the firm of C. and J. Greenwood, whose surveys—described in J. B. Harley, *Christopher Greenwood County Map-Maker* (1962) — extended to most of England and Wales. Together with the maps of their rivals, such as those of Andrew Bryant, they provide a second re-survey of Britain (Figure 7), the bulk of it executed in the 1820s and 1830s, and, moreover, comparable in scale (mainly at one inch to a mile) with the surveys of the period 1750-1800. In addition, in southern England, such maps overlap the publication of the early Ordnance Survey maps, themselves issued in groups of county sheets (Part I Essex, 1805; Part II Devon, 1809 and so on). The cartographic raw materials for the local history of the early nineteenth century are especially rich. Not until the 1830s was the published area of Ordnance Survey sheets sufficiently large to really bite into the market of the county surveyor. By mid-century he had largely disappeared.

The nineteenth century also saw a continuing proliferation of small-scale county maps. They illustrated numerous guides and gazetteers, recorded the expansion of the railway network, and even served sporting gentlemen as in *Hobson's fox hunting atlases*. Many new maps were engraved, and numerous lithographic transfers taken from existing plates. The decorative county map was on the wane—although the work of Thomas Moule, a writer on heraldry and antiquities, and first published in *The English Counties Delineated* (1836), was an exception—and the majority reflect the more functional style of the Ordnance Survey. The county maps published in the rival *New English Atlases* of John Cary and Charles Smith, issued in the first decade of the century, are perhaps especially noteworthy in this respect. They provide an edited and standardised version of the late-eighteenth century surveys prepared by many hands. Such derived maps, based progressively on Ordnance Survey data, flourished till the end of the century—indeed beyond—although printed bibliography has often taken 1900 as its terminus.

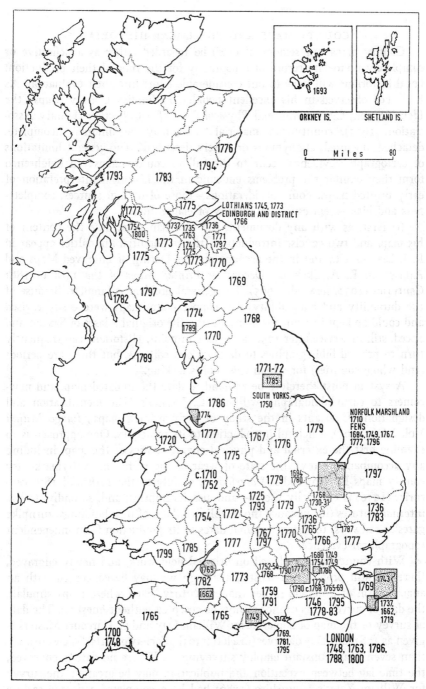

FIGURE 6. County and Major District Maps Published in the Eighteenth Century at a Scale of *Circa* One Inch to one Mile or Over.

County maps can seldom (if ever) be regarded either as a definitive or completely up-to-date record of topography for the time of their production. Local historians will have to put considerable effort into their evaluation. As R. J. Lee observed in his excellent booklet on *English County Maps: the Identification, Cataloguing and Physical Care of a Collection* (Library Association, 1955), county-map material ' . . . may be unique, incomplete, detached, doctored, anonymous or falsely described'. The general limitations of cartographic evidence occur to the full in county maps: in heightened form they exhibit the problems endemic in the historical interpretation of early printed maps. Four considerations—those of dating, sources, completeness and bias—seem especially worthy of elaboration.

(i) First, as with any document, the historian must *date* the content of his map, and two concise introductions to the potential difficulties appear in R. J. Lee, *op. cit.*, and in the account of 'The Dating of Engraved Maps and Atlases' in R. A. Skelton's *Decorative Printed Maps of the 15th to 18th Centuries* (1952, new ed., 1965). The general problem is familiar. Because of the durability and adaptability of a copper plate, maps were easily revised and could be kept in print for many years: the original atlases of Saxton and Speed, still in service after 1750, are a case in point. Historians can frequently turn to printed bibliographies to date various editions, but there are periods (and whole counties) for which this tool is lacking.

A system must therefore be at hand to date the undated map, and newcomers to carto-bibliography will find C. Verner's 'The identification and designation of variants in the study of early printed maps', *Imago Mundi* Vol. XIX (1965), a helpful introduction to its principles. One approach is to examine first the *external* and physical characteristics of the map, including any accompanying text, the state of wear of the plate, the watermark—for county maps E. Heawood's *Watermarks, mainly of the 17th and 18th centuries* (1950) is especially useful—and also its imprint; and, secondly, to use *internal* features (for instance the established dates of new buildings, turnpike gates or railways) to assign terminal dates to its production from independent topographical evidence.

With county surveys based on original field work, and newly engraved, there are still problems of dating, although we may be concerned with an anachronism of a decade rather than a century. Even where maps stipulate the date of survey, this cannot always be accepted without question. The date of survey of the map of Somerset by William Day and C. Harcourt Masters is given as 1782, but Day observes (in a letter to the Society of Arts) 'We were more than seven years constant employ surveying it'. Where no date is engraved, the time lag between execution and publication may be greater: the survey for William Yates's Lancashire (1786) had been completed a decade earlier; and (an extreme case) John Strachey's survey of Somerset (1736) lasted for a

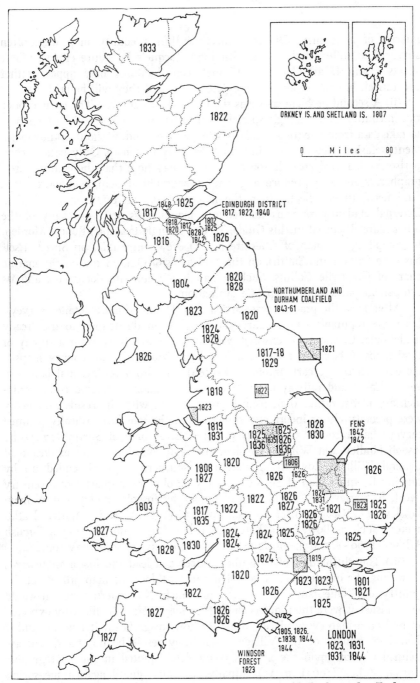

FIGURE 7. County and Major District Maps Published in the Early Nineteenth Century at a Scale of *Circa* One Inch to One Mile or Over.

quarter of a century. Different sheets within a county map were often surveyed at different dates, as with John Rocque's Berkshire (1761), where sheets I and II are dated 1752. Such considerations may appear rather theoretical, but where an accurate date is required they will be critical.

(ii) A second problem concerns the map-maker's *sources*. The normal practice in county map-making, especially with small-scale commercial atlases, was to take data from one (or several) existing sources, and, without acknowledgement, refashion the material into an apparently new map. Only patient comparison will reveal possible sources and we may note that the county cartographer, aiming to produce a general topographical map, had more scope (and need) to be eclectic than the maker of say an estate or canal plan. External evidence confirms that county map-makers drew on many of the other maps discussed in this *Guide*. To cite a single example, Robert Morden, in compiling his map of Cheshire (1695) drew, *inter alia*, on Speed (itself based on Saxton and Smith), on the road maps of Ogilby, and on the marine chart of Greenvile Collins. Such a map is a composite document, and its component parts require separate evaluation.

After 1700 the practice was carried into the age of more detailed surveys. Even the reputable county surveyor was seldom disinclined to use 'ready made' data. C. and J. Greenwood went so far as to advertise for a supply of local maps. Estate plans were liable to be incorporated into county maps— more so where the cartographer (as often) was also a professional land surveyor. Canal and railway details were also commonly inserted from Parliamentary plans, rather than from ground survey, with the result that many were prematurely or incorrectly shown. Even the most scientifically planned surveys had recourse to secondary materials. A map of Surrey (1793), by Joseph Lindley and William Crosley, although conceived as an extension of General William Roy's triangulation in southern England, ended up by copying Rocque's map of Surrey—already obsolete by a quarter of a century (see J. B. Harley, ' . . . The Map of Surrey by Joseph Lindley and William Crosley', *The Geographical Journal* Vol. 132 (1966)). And commercial atlas makers, such as Bowen and Kitchin, in *The Large* and *The Royal English Atlases* (1760 - c. 1763), continued to draw entirely on secondary sources.

(iii) The elucidation of date and sources can lead the historian towards answering the question 'How complete a record does the map provide of the countryside?' One danger is to expect too much. No modern historian would be so misled as were the nineteenth-century map-users who allegedly expected 'to find on a map every place, no matter how insignificant it may be; and if their own hamlet or the Village where they reside be not set down, are inclined to look upon the map as incomplete' (quoted in the *Cartographic Journal* Vol. 4 (1967), p. 15). Equally, we must guard against measuring county maps too inflexibly against the yardstick of the Ordnance Survey Seventh Series one-inch maps. This may induce us to ignore deliberately imposed limits of scale and convention, or to repeat the error (for instance) of G. H. Dury in *The East Midlands and the Peak* (1963) who used eighteenth-century maps to show rural settlement patterns without considering that, amongst isolated settlements, they purported to show only the main 'gentlemen's seats' and farmhouses.

There are several other ways to assess reality in the map. As with all maps, the reconstruction of methods of survey, drafting, and engraving, is helpful in understanding the end product. The surviving evidence of these techniques is uneven. The rough notebooks of a surveyor, as preserved for John Warburton's Yorkshire, 1720 (B. M. Lansdowne MS 895), and discussed by W. B. Crump in 'The genesis of Warburton's "Map of Yorkshire", 1720', *Thoresby Society Miscellanea* Vol. 28 (1928), remind us (in this case) that maps based on road traverse are progressively unreliable away from these roads. Surveyor's accounts of their own work vary in usefulness. Few can match the frankness of *Norden's Preparative to His Speculum Britanniae*, in which he answers point by point the criticisms of his county surveying. In a less valuable category are the 'Memoirs' printed by several county surveyors—as M. J. Armstrong's for his map of Peebles, 1795—but which sought to present the work in a favourable light; similarly, prospectuses issued as broadsheets or in newspapers are, by their nature as advertising matter, biased documents. A useful antidote occurs in the critical comments of well-informed contemporary map-users. Richard Gough, for example, writing in 1780, had asserted ' . . . there is scarce a single one that does not abound with faults, and a set of county maps remains to be hoped for from the undertakers of surveys of counties'; while Arthur Young had dismissed John Kirby's map of Suffolk (1736) with unusual terseness as 'a miserable one'. William Mudge and Isaac Dalby, too, in prosecuting the early trigonometrical survey of Great Britain, had commented in 1799 on 'the very erroneous state of our maps', although it may be noted that they had in mind geodetic rather than topographical accuracy.

An important tool of evaluation is the comparison of topography on a county map with other independent sources. F. G. Emmison illustrates the method in several studies of Essex maps, by checking their detail against contemporary estate plans. John Rocque's 'An Exact Survey of the Citys of London Westminster . . . and the Country near ten miles round' (1744-46) was unreliable: 'Comparison with numerous contemporary MS maps of Essex estates proves that many features are untrustworthy and field boundaries are largely fictitious' (*County Maps of Essex 1576-1853, a Handlist* (1955)). On the other hand, similar tests applied to John Chapman's and Peter André's map of Essex (1777) revealed it as remarkably accurate: 'The surveyors would have been justifiably pleased, had they known that their work, when extensively checked with large-scale contemporary estate maps nearly two centuries later, stood the test' (A *Reproduction of a Map of the County of Essex 1777*, Essex Record Office, 1950).

(iv) A final consideration concerns the element of bias or of the subjective preferences as the total character of the landscape he surveyed. This is where in all county maps. Their content may reflect as much a surveyor's personal local historians, by uncovering the biographies of local surveyors, could throw much-needed light on the strength and weaknesses of particular maps. As other men map-makers were influenced by their social and economic environment. At its simplest we can safely say that one county surveyor may have had a different eye for country, for detail, for accuracy, than the next. It would be surprising if a surveyor living on one of our coalfields in the early railway age chose to emphasise the same aspects of landscape as a man trained in the countryside of southern England a century earlier. Instances of bias, conscious or unconscious, are legion. Some cartographers like John Speed were antiquarians interested in historical features, but others, like Robert Plot, were natural scientists. Isaac Taylor was a keen amateur archaeologist— and some of his county maps, including Dorset (1765), provide the fullest distribution of field antiquities before the Ordnance Survey. John Rocque, on the other hand, whose original trade was a *dessinateur des jardins*, paid little attention to archaeological features, yet obviously set store by the prominent depiction of parks, plantations, and other aspects of land use on his maps. Prejudice could creep into the county as well as to the political map. The advice given to John Strachey, when revising his map of Somerset for publication, was that the house of a certain Mr. Holloway, 'a Quaker of Bridgwater formerly a joyner, now a Master Builder . . . of 3 little Rooms on the Floor and 2 Stories high which . . . He calls a Pavilion and would place it amongst Gentlemen's Seats, . . . methinks is of little consequence and not worthy a place in your Map'.

Map-makers then, like map-users today, were invariably human. The historian must recognise that many maps have more of the qualities of a portrait than of a photograph. They are as much perceived as measured, and may embody concepts about the real world at the same time as they attempt to record its factual detail. But in the study of the past ways of looking at things are often as important as the things themselves. Even the geographical deficiencies of early maps can cast light on the attitudes and intellectual background of the age and locality in which they were made.

7 Bibliographical postscript

This list of references, designed to supplement those incorporated in the text, consists either of publications which have appeared since the original articles were compiled, or of a lesser number of older items, missing from the narrative. References in the text are not repeated, unless they are of major general importance. Where it is not stated the place of publication is London. I am grateful to Mr. Robin V. Clarke for help in compiling this bibliography.

1. GENERAL BACKGROUND TO THE HISTORY OF BRITISH CARTOGRAPHY

Bagley, J. J., 'County Maps and Town Plans' in *Historical Interpretation 2: Sources of English History 1540 to the Present Day* (1971), 173-87

Bagrow, L., *History of Cartography* (1964). Revised and enlarged by R. A. Skelton.

Bricker, C., *Landmarks of Mapmaking: An illustrated survey of maps and mapmakers*. Maps chosen and displayed by R. V. Tooley, text by C. Bricker, preface by G. R. Crone (Amsterdam, 1968). (London edition: *A History of Cartography*, 1969)

British Museum, *Guide to the Catalogue of the British Museum Exhibition 'The Mapping of Britain'* (1964)

Brown, L. A., *The Story of Maps* (Boston, USA, 1949)

Crone, G. R., 'The Mapping of the British Isles' in J. W. Watson and J. B. Sissons (eds.) *The British Isles: a systematic geography* (1964), 40-52

Crone, G. R., *Maps and their makers: an introduction to the history of cartography*, 4th ed. (1968)

Fordham, H. G., *Some Notable Surveyors & Map-Makers of the Sixteenth, Seventeenth & Eighteenth centuries and their Work: a study in the history of cartography* (Cambridge, 1929)

Harley, J. B., 'Uncultivated Fields in the History of British Cartography', *Cart. Journ.* 4 (1967), 7-11

Inglis, H. R. G. (ed.), *The Early Maps of Scotland*, 2nd edition (Edinburgh, Royal Scottish Geographical Society, 1936)

Lister, R., *How to Identify Old Maps and Globes, with a List of Cartographers, Engravers, Publishers and Printers Concerned with Printed Maps and Globes from c. 1500 to c. 1850* (1965)

Lynam, E., *British Maps and Map-Makers* (1944)

Lynam, E., *The Mapmaker's Art: Essays on the History of Maps* (1953)

Robinson, A. H. W., *Marine Cartography in Britain. A History of the Sea Chart to 1855* (Leicester, Leicester University Press, 1962)

Skelton, R. A., *Decorative Printed Maps of the 15th to 18th Centuries.* Revised edition of Old Decorative Maps and Charts by A. L. Humphreys (1926), new text (1952, reprinted 1965)

Thompson, F. M. L., *Chartered Surveyors: the growth of a profession* (1968)

Tooley, R. V., *Maps and Map-Makers.* Third edition (1970)

Tooley, R. V., *A Dictionary of Mapmakers* (London, Map Collectors' Circle, Map Collectors' Series nos. 16 (1965), 28 (1966), 40 (1967), 50 (1968), 67 (1970) . . . in progress)

2. BIBLIOGRAPHIES AND CATALOGUES OF MAPS

Adams, I. H., *Scottish Record Office: Descriptive List of Plans*, 2 vols. (Edinburgh, HMSO, 1966 and 1970)

Bonser, K. G. and Nichols, H., *Printed maps and plans of Leeds, 1711-1900*, (Leeds, The Thoresby Society, 1960)

British Museum, *The British Museum Catalogue of Printed Maps, Charts and Plans*, 15 vols. (1967)

Butcher, N. E., *The History and Development of Geological Cartography. Catalogue of the Exhibition of Geological Maps in the University Library* (Reading, 1967)

Campbell, T., *Catalogue 6 Maps. Outline of the British Isles: Printed Maps 1482-1887* (London, Weinreb & Douwma, 1970)

Catalogues of Plans of Abandoned Mines, Vols. 1-5, Supplements (Mines Department of the Board of Trade, HMSO, 1928-1939). A series of printed regional catalogues of mine plans now deposited in various archives of the National Coal Board

Chubb, T., 'A Descriptive Catalogue of the Printed Maps of Wiltshire from 1576 to the publication of the 25in. Ordnance Survey, 1855', *Wiltshire Archaeological and Natural History Magazine*, 37 (Devizes, 1911), 211-317

Chubb, T., *A Descriptive Catalogue of the Printed Maps of Gloucestershire, 1577-1911.* Bristol and Gloucestershire Archaeological Society (Bristol, 1912)

Chubb, T., *A Descriptive List of the Printed Maps of Somersetshire 1575-1914*, Somerset Archaeological and Natural History Society (1914)

Chubb, T. and Stephen, G. H., *A Descriptive List of the Printed Maps of Norfolk, 1574-1916: Descriptive List of Norwich Plans, 1541-1914* (Norwich, 1928)

Cubbon, A. M., *Early Maps of the Isle of Man: A Guide to the Collection in the Manx Museum* (Douglas, The Manx Museum and National Trust, 3rd edition, 1967)

Curwen, J. F., 'The chorography, or a descriptive catalogue of the printed maps of Cumberland and Westmorland', *Trans. Cumberland and Westmorland Antiquarian and Archaeological Society*, N.S. 18 (1918), 1-92

Darlington, I. and Howgego, J., *The Printed Maps of London, circa 1553-1850* (1964)

Dickinson, P. G. M., *Maps in the County Record Office, Huntingdon* (St. Ives, Imray Laurie, Norrie and Wilson Ltd., 1968)

English, B. A. (ed.), *Handlist of West Riding Enclosure Awards* (National Register of Archives West Riding [Northern Section] Committee, South Yorkshire Committee, 1965)

Evans, O. C., *Marine Plans and Charts of Wales* (London, Map Collectors' Circle, Map Collectors' Series No. 54 [1969])

Eyles, J. M., 'William Smith (1769-1839): A Bibliography of his Published Writings, Maps and Geological Sections, Printed and Lithographed', *Journ. of the Society for the Bibliography of Natural History* 5 (1969), 87-109

Harvey, P. D. A. and Thorpe, H., *The Printed Maps of Warwickshire, 1576-1900* (Warwick, 1959)

Hodson, D., *The Printed Maps of Hertfordshire, 1577-1900*, 3 vols. (London, Map Collectors' Circle, Map Collectors' Series, nos. 53 and 59, 1969, and 65, 1970)

Hyde, R., *Ward Maps of the City of London* (London, Map Collectors' Circle, Map Collectors' Series, no. 38, 1967)

Hyde, R., 'The Printed Maps of London, 1851-1900' (Library Association Thesis, 1970)

Koeman, C., *Atlantes Neerlandici. Bibliography of terrestrial, maritime and celestial atlases and pilot books, published in the Netherlands up to 1880*, 3 vols. (Amsterdam, Theatrum Orbis Terrarum, vol. 1, 1967, 2 and 3, 1969)

National Maritime Museum, *Catalogue of the Library*. Vol. 3 (2 pt.), *Atlases & Cartography* (1971)

Newcastle University Library, *A Catalogue of an Exhibition of Old Maps of North-East England, 1600-1865* (Newcastle upon Tyne, 1967). Library Publications. Extra Series No. 8

Ordnance Survey, *Catalogue of Photographs of Old Cadastral and other Plans of Great Britain* (Southampton, 1935)

Price, U., 'The maps of Buckinghamshire 1574-1800', *Records of Buckinghamshire* 15 (1947-51), 107-33, 182-207, 250-69

Public Record Office, *Maps and Plans in the Public Record Office, I. British Isles, c. 1410-1860* (1967)

79

Quixley, R. C. E., *Antique Maps of Cornwall and the Isles of Scilly* (Penzance, The Author, 1966)

Rodger, E. M., *The Large-Scale County Maps of the British Isles, 1596-1850: a Union List*. 2nd edition (Oxford, Bodleian Library, 1972)

Sharp, H. A., *An Historical Catalogue of Surrey Maps* (Croydon, 1929)

Skelton, R. A. and Harvey, P. D. A., 'Local Maps and Plans before 1500', *Journ. of the Society of Archivists* 3 (1969), 496-7

Skelton, R. A., *County Atlases of the British Isles, 1579-1850. A Bibliography. 1579-1703* (1970)

Skelton, R. A., *The maps of a Tudor statesman* (Oxford, Roxburghe Club, 1971)

Smith, B. S., 'The Dougharty Family of Worcester, Estate Surveyors and Mapmakers, 1700-60. Catalogue of Maps and Plans by the Dougharty Family. *Worcestershire Historical Society Miscellany II, New Series 5* (Worcester, 1967), 138-80

Walne, P., *A Catalogue of Manuscript Maps in Hertfordshire Record Office* (Hertford, Hertfordshire County Council, 1969)

Whitaker, H., *A Descriptive List of the Printed Maps of Yorkshire and Its Ridings, 1577-1900. Yorkshire Archaeological Society Record Series 86* (Leeds, 1933)

Whitaker, H., *A Descriptive List of the Printed Maps of Lancashire, 1577-1900* (Manchester, Chetham Society, N.S. 101, 1938)

Whitaker, H., *A Descriptive List of the Printed Maps of Cheshire, 1577-1900* (Manchester, Chetham Society, N.S. 106, 1942)

Whitaker, H., *A Descriptive List of the Printed Maps of Northamptonshire, 1576-1900. Northamptonshire Record Society 14* (Northampton, 1948)

Whitaker, H., *A Descriptive List of the Maps of Northumberland, 1576-1900* (Newcastle upon Tyne, Society of Antiquaries, 1949)

Verner, C., *Captain Collins' Coasting Pilot: A Carto-Bibliographical Analysis* (London, Map Collectors' Circle, Map Collectors' Series no. 58, 1969)

3. OTHER REFERENCES

Adams, I. H., 'The Scottish Record Office Plan Collection', *Cart. Journ.* 4 (1967), 28

Adams, I. H., 'Large-scale Manuscript Plans in Scotland', *Journ. of the Society of Archivists*, 3 (1967), 286-90

Adams, I. H., 'The Land Surveyor and his Influence on the Scottish Rural Landscape', *Scott. Geog. Mag.* 84 (1968), 248-55

Baptist, Sister M., 'Eighteenth-Century Maps and Estate Plans of Bromley, Beckenham and Penge', *Archaeologia Cantiana*, 81 (Maidstone, 1967), 31-8

Bassett, D. A., *A Source-Book of Geological, Geomorphological and Soil Maps for Wales and the Welsh Borders (1800-1965)*. (Cardiff, National Museum of Wales, 1967) de Boer, G. and Skelton, R. A., 'The Earliest English Chart with Soundings', *Imago Mundi* 23 (Amsterdam, N. Israel, 1969), 9-16

Bull, G. B. G., 'Thomas Milne's Land Utilisation Map of the London Area in 1800', *Geog. Journ.* 122 (1956), 25-30

Campbell, E. M. J., 'An English Philosophico-Chorographical Chart', *Imago Mundi* 6 (Stockholm, Kartografiska Sällskapet, 1949), 79-84.

Campbell, E. M. J., 'The Beginnings of the Characteristic Sheet to English Maps', *Geog. Journ.* 128 (1962), 411-15

Carpenter, A. M., 'The Value of the Tithe Surveys to the Study of Land Ownership and Occupancy in the Mid-Nineteenth Century, with Special Reference to South Hertfordshire', *Hertfordshire Past and Present* 7 (Hitchin, Hertfordshire Local History Council, 1967), 48-52

Carr, A. P., 'The Growth of Orford Spit: Cartographic and Historical Evidence from the Sixteenth Century', *Geog. Journ.* 135 (1969), 28-39

Chambers, B., 'M. J. Armstrong in Norfolk: the Progress of an Eighteenth-Century County Survey', *Geog. Journ.* 130 (1964), 427-31

Clarke, R. V., 'The Use of Watermarks in Dating Old Series One-Inch Maps', *Cart. Journ.* 6 (1969), 114-29. (This study has important applications to other nineteenth-century printed maps)

Close, C., 'The Old English Mile', *Geog. Journ.* 76 (1930), 338-42

Close, C., *The Early Years of the Ordnance Survey* (Chatham, Institution of the Royal Engineers, 1926). New edition with introduction by J. B. Harley (Newton Abbot, David & Charles, 1969)

Crone, G. R., 'Early Mapping of the British Isles', *Scott. Geog. Mag.* 78 (1962), 73-80

Crone, G. R., 'Early Cartographic Activity in Britain', *Geog. Journ.* 128 (1962), 406-10

Crosby Public Libraries, *Local Maps and Documents* (Great Crosby, 1967)

Dilke, O. A., 'Roman Surveying and Centuriation in Britain' in *The Roman Land Surveyors: An Introduction to the Agrimensores* (Newton Abbot, 1971)

Duckham, B. F., 'Turnpike Records', *History* 53 (1968), 217-20.

East, W. G., 'Land Utilisation at the end of the Eighteenth Century', *Geog. Journ.* 85 (1937), 156-72

Evans, G. L., 'Richard Norwood, Surveyor, of Stephenage', *Hertfordshire Past and Present* 8 (Hitchin, Hertfordshire Local History Council, 1968), 29-32

Fairhurst, H., 'An Old Estate Plan of Auchindrain, Mid-Argyll', *Scottish Studies* 12 (Edinburgh, 1968), 183-7

Flower, R., 'Laurence Nowell and the Discovery of England in Tudor Times', *Proceedings of the British Academy* 21 (1935), 47-73

Fordham, H. G., 'Saxton's General Map of England and Wales', *Geog. Journ.* 67 (1926), 63-6

Fordham, H. G., 'Christopher Saxton of Dunnmgley. His Life and Work' Thoresby Society's *Miscellanea*, 28 (Leeds, 1928), 356-84; additional note *ibid.*, 491. Reprinted in J. M. Henshall, *Sir H. George Fordham, Carto-Bibliographer* (London, Map Collectors' Circle, Map Collectors' Series no. 51, 1969)

Fordham, H. G., 'Some Surveys and Maps of the Elizabethan Period remaining in Manuscript. Saxton, Symonson and Norden', *Geog. Journ.* 71 (1928), 50-60

Harley, J. B., 'The Bankruptcy of Thomas Jefferys: an Episode in the Economic History of Eighteenth Century Map-Making', *Imago Mundi* 20 (Amsterdam, N. Israel, 1966), 27-48

Harley, J. B., 'The Evaluation of Early Maps: towards a Methodology', *Imago Mundi* 22 (Amsterdam, N. Israel, 1968), 62-74

Harley, J. B., 'The Ordnance Survey and the Origins of Official Geological Mapping in Devon and Cornwall', in *Exeter Essays in Geography* ed. by K. J. Gregory and W. L. D. Ravenhill (Exeter, 1971), 105-23

Harley, J. B. and Ravenhill, W. L. D., 'Proposals for County Maps of Cornwall (1699) and Devon (1700)', *Devon and Cornwall Notes and Queries* 32 (Exeter, 1971), 33-9.

Harvey, P. D. A., 'A 13th Century Plan from Waltham Abbey, Essex', *Imago Mundi* 22 (Amsterdam, N. Israel, 1968), 10-12

Heawood, E., 'Saxton's Large Map of England', *Geog. Journ.* 76 (1930), 86-7

Hind, A. M., *Engraving in England in the Sixteenth and Seventeenth Centuries. Part I The Tudor period* (Cambridge, 1952); *Part II The reign of James I* (Cambridge, 1955)

Jeacock, S. and Wallis, H., 'Political Arithmetic', *Cart. Journ.* 7 (1970), 9

Kenney, C. E., *The Quadrant and the Quill. A book written in honour of Captain Samuel Sturmy 'a tryed and trusty Sea-man', and author of The Mariner's Magazine 1669* (1947)

Kerr, B., 'Dorset Fields and Their Names'. *Proceedings Dorset Natural History and Archaeological Society* 89 (Dorchester, 1968), 233-68

Kiely, E. R., *Surveying Instruments, their history and classroom use* (New York, 1947). National Council of Teachers of Mathematics, Nineteenth Yearbook

Kinniburgh, I. A. G., 'A Note on Timothy Pont's Survey of Scotland', *Scottish Studies* (Edinburgh, 1968), 187-9

Koeman, C., 'Some new contributions to the knowledge of Blaeu atlases', *Tijdschrift van het Koninklijk Nederlansch Aardrijkskundig Genootschap* (1960), 278-86

Koeman, C., 'Levels of historical evidence in early maps (with examples)', *Imago Mundi* 22 (Amsterdam, N. Israel, 1968), 75-80

Kosinski, L. A., 'Exhibit of Early Distribution Maps in the British Museum', *Geog. Rev.* 60 (New York, 1970), 267-9

Lambert, A., 'The Agriculture of Oxfordshire at the end of the eighteenth century', *Agricultural History* 29 (1955), 31-8

Lambert, A., 'Early Maps and Local Studies', *Geography* 61 (1956), 166-77

Lebon, J. H. G., 'Old Maps and Rural Change in Ayrshire', *Scott. Geog. Mag.* 68 (Edinburgh, 1952), 104-9

Lewarne, J. G. W., 'A Cartographical Survey of the Area. XII: Fetcham Enclosure Award, 1813', *Proc. Leatherhead & Dist. Local Hist. Soc.* 3 (1967), 14-18

Lobel, M. D., 'The Value of Early Maps as Evidence for the Topography of English Towns', *Imago Mundi* 22 (Amsterdam, N. Israel, 1968), 50-61

Lock, C. B. M., *Modern Maps and Atlases: An Outline Guide to Twentieth Century Production* (1969)

Lynam, E. W., 'English Maps and Map-makers of the Sixteenth Century', *Geog. Journ.* 116 (1950), 7-28. Reprinted in *The Map-maker's Art* (1953)

Megaw, B. R. S., 'The Date of Pont's survey and its background', *Scottish Studies* 13 (Edinburgh, 1969), 71-4

Moir, A. L., *The World Map in Hereford Cathedral* (Hereford, The Cathedral, 5th edition, 1970)

Mountfield, S., 'Captain Greenvile Collins and Mr. Pepys', *The Mariner's Mirror* 56 (Cambridge, 1970), 85-97

Munby, L. M., 'Tithe Apportionments and Maps', *History* 54 (1969), 68-71

Newton, K. C., 'The Walkers of Essex', *Bulletin of the Society of University Cartographers* 4 (1969-70), 1-6

North, F. J., 'The Map of Wales', *Archaeologia Cambrensis* 90 (1935), 1-69

Osley, A. S., *Mercator: a monograph on the lettering of maps* (1969)

Osley, A. S., 'Calligraphy—a Cartographic Tool?', *Imago Mundi* 24 (Amsterdam, N. Israel, 1970), 63-75

Raistrick, A., *Yorkshire Maps and Map-Makers* (Clapham, via Lancaster, The Dalesman Publishing Company, 1969)

Ravenhill, W. L. D., 'The Newly-Discovered Manuscript Maps of Cornwall by John Norden', *Geog. Journ.* 136 (1970), 593-5

Ravenhill, W. L. D., 'John Norden's Maps of Cornwall: A Problem in the Historical Cartography of South-West England', *Cart. Journ.* 7 (1970), 89-90

Ravenhill, W. L. D., 'The Missing Maps from John Norden's Survey of Cornwall' in *Exeter Essays in Geography* ed. by K. J. Gregory and W. L. D. Ravenhill (Exeter, 1971), 93-104

Rawnsley, J. E., *Antique Maps of Yorkshire and Their Makers* (Guiseley, near Leeds, The Author, 1970)

Roberts, B. K., 'An Early Tudor Sketch Map', *History Studies* I (1968), 33-8

Robinson, A. H., 'The Genealogy of the Isopleth', *Cart. Journ.* 8 (1971), 49-53

Robinson, E., 'The Profession of Civil Engineer in the Eighteenth Century . . . ' in A. E. Musson and E. Robinson, *Science and Technology in the Industrial Revolution* (Manchester, Manchester University Press, 1969), 372-392

Rostenberg, L., *English Publishers in the Graphic Arts, 1599-1700* (New York, 1963)

Shelby, L. R., *John Rogers: Tudor Military Engineer* (Oxford, Clarendon Press, 1967)

Skelton, R. A., 'The Royal Map Collections of England', *Imago Mundi* 13 ('S'Gravenage, Mouton & Co., 1956), 181-3

Skelton, R. A., 'The Military Survey of Scotland, 1747-1755', *Scott. Geog. Mag.* 83 (Edinburgh), 1967), 5-16. Also as The Royal Scottish Geographical Society Special Publication No. 1

Skelton, R. A., 'The Military Surveyor's Contribution to British Cartography in the 16th Century', *Imago Mundi* 24 (Amsterdam, N. Israel, 1970), 77-83

Smith, B. S., 'The business archives of estate agents', *Journ. Soc. Archivists* 3 (1967), 298-300

Smith, T. R., 'Nicholas Comberford, Seventeenth-century Chart-maker at the "Signe of the Platt" in Ratcliff', *Imago Mundi* 24 (Amsterdam, N. Israel, 1970), 95

Steed, V. W., *Notes on an Exhibition of Maps Illustrating the Historical Development of Wychwood Forest and North Oxfordshire* (Oxford, Ashmolean Museum, 1968)

Steer, F. W., 'A Dictionary of Land Surveyors in Britain', *Cart. Journ.* 4 (1967), 124-6

Stone, J. C., 'An Evaluation of the "Nidisdaile" Manuscript Map by Timothy Pont: Implications for the Role of the Gordons in the Preparation of the Blaeu Maps of Scotland', *Scott. Geog. Mag.* 84 (Edinburgh, 1968), 160-71

Stone, J. C., 'The Preparation of the Blaeu Maps of Scotland: a Further Assessment', *Scott. Geog. Mag.* 86 (Edinburgh, 1970), 16-24

Storrie, M. C., 'William Bald, F.R.S.E., c. 1789-1857; Surveyor, Cartographer and Civil Engineer', Institute of British Geographers, *Transactions and Papers* 47 (1969), 205-31

Taylor, A. B., 'Name Studies in Sixteenth-century Scottish Maps', *Imago Mundi* 19 (Amsterdam, N. Israel, 1965), 113-15

Taylor, E. G. R., *The Mathematical Practitioners of Hanoverian England, 1714-1840* (Cambridge, 1966)

Thomas, C., 'Estate Surveys as Sources in Historical Geography', *Nat. Lib. Wales Journ.* 14 (1966), 451-68

Twyman, M., *Lithography 1800-1850* (1970)

Wallis, H. and Jeacock, S., 'Royal United Services Institution Map Collection', *Cart. Journ.* 7 (1970), 39-40

Walters, G., 'Themes in the Large-Scale Mapping of Wales in the Eighteenth Century', *Cart. Journ.* 5 (1968), 135-46

Walters, G., 'Engraved Maps from the English Topographies c. 1660-1825' *Cart. Journ.* 7 (1970), 81-8

Walters, G., 'The Morrises and the Map of Anglesey', *The Welsh History Review* 5 (1970), 164-71

Warren, K. F., 'Introduction to the map resources of the British Museum', *Professional Geographer* 17 (1965), 1-7

Welch, E., 'The Earliest Maps of Southampton', *Cart. Journ.* 2 (1965), 66-7

Wieder, F. C., *Monumenta Cartographica* vol. III (The Hague, 1929). An account of the atlases and maps of the brothers Blaeu.

4. SOME RECENT FACSIMILES

Andrews, J. and Dury, A., *Map of Wiltshire 1773. A reduced facsimile.* (Devizes, Wiltshire Arch. and Nat. Hist. Soc. Records Branch, 8, 1952)

Andrews, J., Dury, A. and Herbert, W., *A Topographical Map, of the County of Kent in Twenty-Five Sheets, on a Scale of two inches to a Mile . . .* 1769. Facsimile. (Lympne Castle, Kent, H. Margary, 1968)

Bickham, G., *The British Monarchy, or A New Chorographical Description of all the Dominions Subject to the King of Great Britain.* Facsimile of the second edition 1748-1754. (Newcastle upon Tyne, Frank Graham, 1967)

Blaeu, W. and J., *Theatrum Orbis Terrarum sive Atlas Novus,* 1648. Facsimiles (Edinburgh, John Bartholomew & Son, 1966 continuing)

Bowen, E., *Britannia Depicta or Ogilby Improved,* 1720. Facsimile with an Introduction by J. B. Harley. (Newcastle upon Tyne, Frank Graham, 1970)

Bowen, E. and Kitchin, T., *The Royal English Atlas: Eighteenth-Century County Maps of England and Wales.* Facsimile. Introduction by J. B. Harley and Donald Hodson. (Newton Abbot, David & Charles, 1971)

Braun, G. and Hogenberg, F., *Civitates Orbis Terrarum 1572-1618.* 3 vols. Facsimile. Preface by R. V. Tooley. Introduction by R. A. Skelton. (Amsterdam, Theatrum Orbis Terrarum, 1965)

Carew, R., *The Survey of Cornwall. Edited with an Introduction by F. E. Halliday. With 10 maps by John Norden* (1969)

Cole, G. and Roper, J. *Plans of English Towns . . . 1810* (Monmouth, Brian Stevens Historic Prints, 1970)

Crosthwaite, P., *A series of Accurate Maps of the Principal Lakes of Cumberland, Westmorland, and Lancashire . . .* Facsimile. Introduction and notes by W. Rollinson. (Newcastle upon Tyne, Frank Graham, 1968)

Donn, B., *Benjamin Donn: A Map of the County of Devon 1765.* Facsimile. Introduction by W. L. D. Ravenhill. (Exeter, Devon and Cornwall Record Society and The University of Exeter, 1965)

Horwood, R., *Horwood's Plan of London, Westminster, Southwark and Parts Adjoining.* Facsimile. (London Topographical Society, Pub. No. 106, 1966)

Library of Congress, Washington, *Facsimiles of Rare Historical Maps. A List of Reproductions for Sale by Various Publishers and Distributors.* Compiled by W. W. Ristow and M. E. Graziani, 3rd edition (Washington, D.C., 1968)

Lynam, E. W., Introduction to: *An Atlas of England and Wales. The Maps of Christopher Saxton Engraved 1574-1579*. Coloured facsimiles of British Museum Maps c. 7 c. 1 (1934, revised 1939)

Manchester Public Libraries, *Maps of Manchester, 1650-1848*. Facsimiles. (Manchester, Public Libraries Committee, 1969)

Margary, H. (ed.), *Two Hundred and Fifty Years of Map-making in the County of Sussex*. A collection of reproductions of printed maps published between the years 1575 and 1825. With Introductory Notes by R. A. Skelton. (Chichester, 1970)

Mercator-Hondius-Janssonius, *Atlas or A Geographicke Description of the Regions, Countries and Kingdoms of the World* . . . *1636*. 2 vols. Bibliographical Note by R. A. Skelton. (Amsterdam, Theatrum Orbis Terrarum, 1968)

Morden, R., *The County Maps from William Camden's Britannia, 1695*. A facsimile with an introduction by J. B. Harley (Newton Abbot, David and Charles, 1972)

Munster, S., *Sebastian Munster: Cosmographie* . . . *Basel 1550*. With an Introduction by Professor Dr. R. Oehme. (Amsterdam, Theatrum Orbis Terrarum, 1968)

Norden, J., *Orford Ness: a Selection of Maps mainly by John Norden*. Presented to James Alfred Steers. (Cambridge, W. Heffer & Sons, 1966)

Norden, J., *John Norden's Manuscript Maps of Cornwall and its nine hundreds*. Facsimile. Introduction by William Ravenhill (Exeter, University of Exeter, 1972)

Ogilby, J., *Britannia. Volume the First: or, an Illustration of the Kingdom of England and Dominion of Wales* . . . *1675*. Bibliographical Note by J. B. Harley. (Amsterdam, Theatrum Orbis Terrarum, 1970)

Ordnance Survey, *Reprint of the First Edition of the One-Inch Ordnance Survey of England and Wales*. 97 sheets. Edited by J. B. Harley (Newton Abbot, David and Charles, 1969-71)

Robertson, A., *The Great Road from London to Bath & Bristol*. (Monmouth, Brian Stevens, 1970)

Saxton, C., *Saxton's Survey of England and Wales and the Maps from it*. Facsimile of Saxton's Wall-map of 1583. Introduction by R. A. Skelton (with contributions by S. T. M. Newman and A. D. Baxter). (Amsterdam, Imago Mundi Supplement, N. Israel, 1972)

Symonson, P., *A New Description of Kent* . . . *1596*. Facsimile (Southampton, Ordnance Survey, 1968). As published by Stent c. 1650

Yates, W., *A Map of the County of Lancashire, 1786*. Facsimile. Introduction by J. B. Harley. (Liverpool, Historic Society of Lancashire and Cheshire, 1968)

86

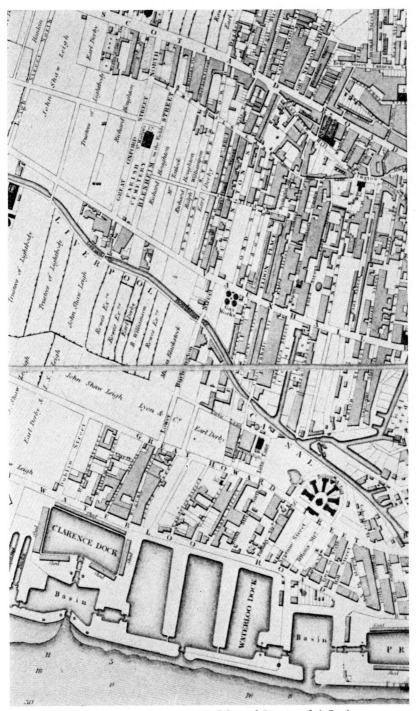

PLATE 1. Part of Jonathan Bennison's Map of Liverpool (1835).
[Reproduced through the courtesy of Liverpool Record Office]

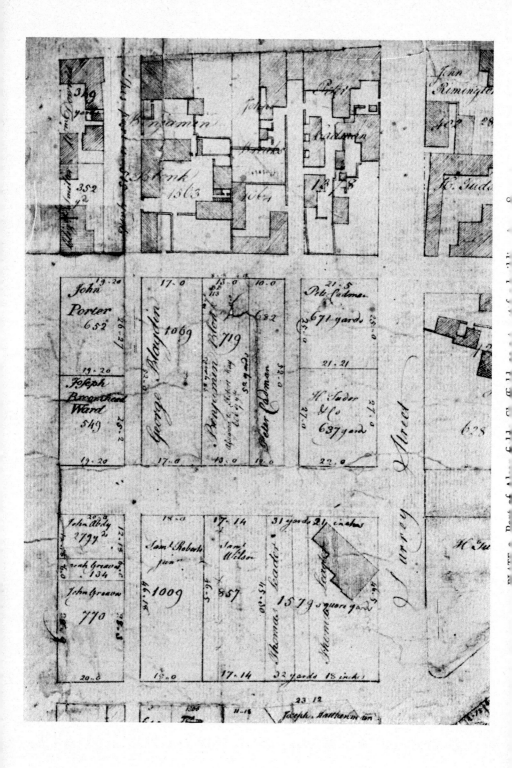

PLATE 9. Part of plan of the Churchfield, 1791, showing the five burgage plots.

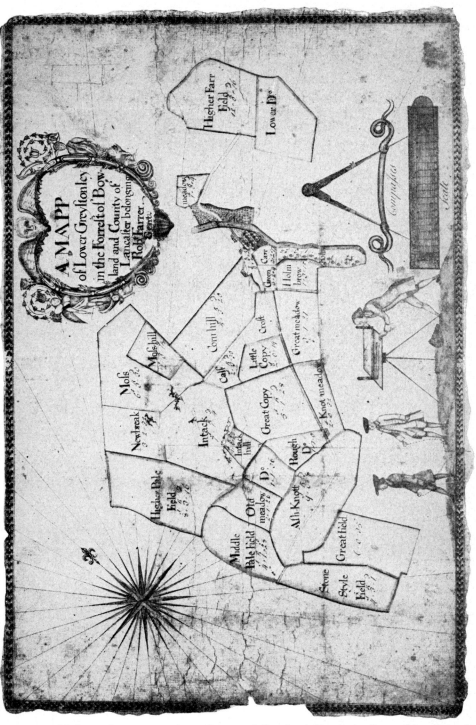

PLATE 3. Eighteenth century plan of part of Bowland Forest in Lancashire Record Office (DDX 19/80).

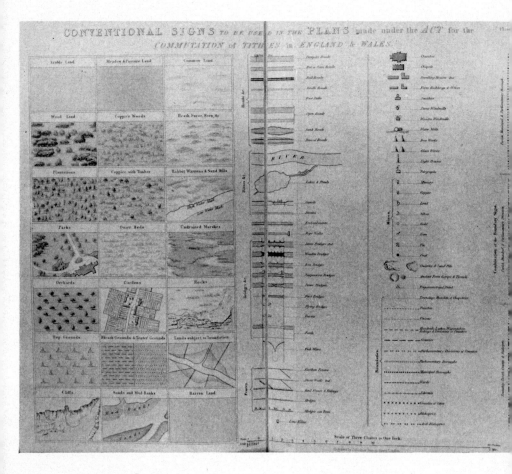

PLATE 4. Conventional signs proposed for use on the Tithe Maps, *c.* 1836, from *Britis* *Parliamentary Paper* 1837 XLI 405.

PLATE 5. A road diversion plan in Sandbach parish, Cheshire. Quarter Sessions File 14th January 1783.

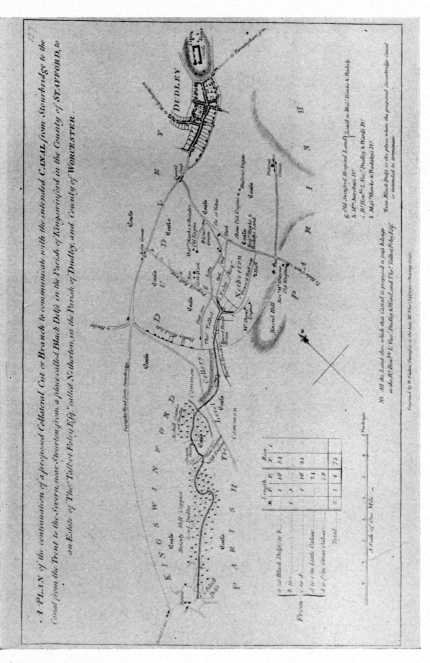

PLATE 6. Eighteenth-century canal plan: a branch from the '… intended Canal from Stourbridge to the Canal from the Trent to the Severn …', c. 1780.

[Reproduced through the courtesy of the Trustees of the British Museum from Maps 4. c. 13. vol. 1 no. 127]

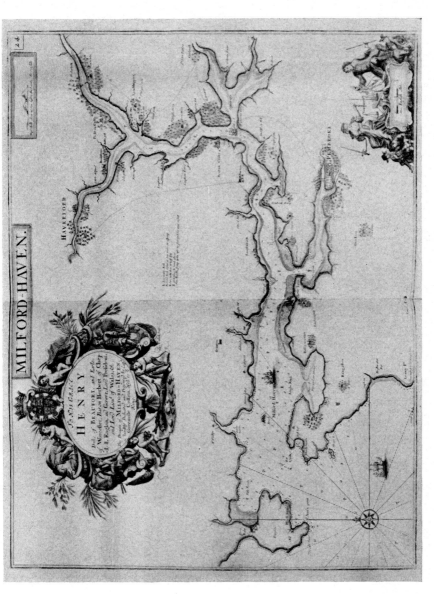

PLATE 7. Milford Haven from Greenvile Collin's *Great Britain's Coasting Pilot* 1693.

PLATE 8. Part of John Ainslie's Map of Forfarshire, surveyed 1794.